JAILING THE
JOHNSTOWN JUDGE

JOE O'KICKI, THE MOB AND CORRUPT JUSTICE

BRUCE SIWY

THE
History
PRESS

Published by The History Press
Charleston, SC
www.historypress.com

First published 2022

Manufactured in the United States

ISBN 9781467152037

Library of Congress Control Number: 2022939464

Organized crime no longer follows the script set forth in the Godfather *series or* Goodfellows. *It has evolved into a pervasive use of legal, banking and business sectors to channel its profits into their pockets and to elect judges, prosecutors, and executives that operate police departments.*

—*Joseph F. O'Kicki, letter to U.S. attorney general Janet Reno, August 25, 1993*

CONTENTS

ACKNOWLEDGEMENTS

I appreciate the trust from J. Banks Smither, The History Press and Arcadia Publishing for helping me to bridge the gap from newsprint to paperback. Reconstructing this wild chapter of Pennsylvania history was done with the help of the following sources: Cambria County president Judge Norman A. Krumenacker III, George Fattman, Sylvia Onusic, Brian Sukenik, Neil Price, Walt Komoroski, Lawrence Claus, Fran Mattre, Lee Wood, Tim Burns, Tony Trigona, Dr. Bill Choby, Rick Kirkham, George B. Kaufman, Frederick T. Martens, Tony Piskurich and Patrick Farabaugh.

My wife, kids, parents and other relatives deserve credit for hearing me out on these topics over the years. Same goes for colleagues at the newspaper: Brian Whipkey for greenlighting the original project; Eric Kieta for asking some of the tough questions; Billy O'Shea for the score; Cody McDevitt for the intro to the business; and Shane Fitzgerald for facilitating the Gannett permissions. Special thanks to Dan Slep and Brenda Carberry at the *Altoona Mirror* for the images and to Ethan Stewart and Dennis Mical, respectively, for the use of 814 Worx and VOMA during interviews.

Dedicated to Babcia, Dziadzio and the rest of the Siwys, who started this thing decades ago with the stories of Uncle Charley.

INTRODUCTION

The swearing-in ceremony—or, as some would whisper, coronation—took place on June 3, 1988, in the Cambria County Courthouse.

Politicians, attorneys and more than three hundred other members of the Ebensburg, Johnstown and surrounding communities filed in shoulder to shoulder to watch Joseph F. O'Kicki become the county's new president judge. Guests included county bar association President E.R. "Mike" Walker, Bishop Joseph V. Adamec of the Diocese of Altoona-Johnstown and the Reverend Ray Streets of the Emmanuel Baptist Church in Richland Township.

Supreme Court of Pennsylvania judge John P. Flaherty was among the speakers. "He is a man of humble beginnings," Flaherty told the audience. "He was born in the village of Parkhill in a home that had no running water. He thereafter attended Franklin High School and was the valedictorian of his graduating class. His father was a coal miner and stone mason who worked on the Roxbury Bandshell in the City of Johnstown.

"Judge O'Kicki has the reputation of being one of the finest jurists, not only in Pennsylvania, but in the United States."

The day was a momentous one for O'Kicki, the son of humble central European immigrants. He'd been a county judge for seventeen years. Now, at the age of fifty-seven, he would replace Judge H. Clifton McWilliams as president judge of Cambria County. McWilliams had just reached the mandatory retirement age of seventy.

Cambria courts given 'alarming' evaluation

By Sandy Ivory
Staff Writer

EBENSBURG — An evaluation report critical of the Cambria County court system was handed over to Joseph F. O'Kicki Friday as he was sworn into office as the county's president judge.

Although details will not be released until O'Kicki has a chance to study the report, state Supreme Court Justice John A. Flaherty said the higher court has been concerned about problems in Cambria for some time.

"Information has reached us about certain areas ... delays and backlogs," Flaherty said. "So we dispatched several top court administrators four months ago to make a survey/analysis

Joseph F. O'Kicki was sworn in as Cambria County president judge Friday.

of the system."

Flaherty indicated he and Chief Supreme Court Justice Robert N.C. Nix conferred on the completed evaluation

and its contents, deciding to turn it over to O'Kicki Friday.

"The findings were not happy findings," Flaherty said of the report. However, he remained vague on specific details, saying only there were problems with long delays involving both civil and criminal cases.

After terming the situation "alarming," Flaherty added that he and the other Supreme Court justices feel O'Kicki can correct the problems.

"We are going to be keeping an eye on Cambria County," Flaherty told reporters. "It is fortunate that Joe is now president judge ... he has the Supreme Court backing and support. Everyone on the court likes Joe O'Kicki."

See **Cambria** on Page A2

The "alarming" condition of Cambria County's court system earned front-page ink in the June 4, 1988 edition of the *Altoona Mirror* newspaper the day after Judge Joseph O'Kicki's swearing-in ceremony as president judge. *Courtesy of the* Altoona Mirror.

With the increased prestige of this position came enormous challenges. Amid his adulation for O'Kicki, Flaherty characterized Cambria County's court system as being in an "alarming" state. He announced that an evaluation of the problems plaguing the system had been completed by several top court administrators with the Administrative Office of Pennsylvania Courts under the direction of Dr. Donald Harris.

"Up until this moment, that study has been kept confidential. I have been authorized, after I have performed the oath, to present you with a copy of this study, investigation and analysis for your review," Flaherty said. "You are accepting a most significant task. Because of that, we want you to know that you will have the strong support and backing of the Supreme Court of Pennsylvania, our administrative office and the chief justices and justices individually in the performance of your task."

Flaherty told reporters later that day, "We are going to be keeping an eye on Cambria County. It is fortunate that Joe is now president judge.... He has the Supreme Court backing and support. Everyone on the court likes Joe O'Kicki."

O'Kicki—a lifelong Democrat who had changed his registration to Republican two years prior in 1986—responded to Flaherty's speech with his own comments on the study and the need for him and his fellow judges to resist influence from powerful outside forces.

"[Do] not allow machines or individuals to adversely influence our judicial system, especially a few of those who would like to place themselves above the law…who employ tools of lies and deceit, merely to accomplish their ends," O'Kicki said. "[Insist] upon justice for your fellow-man."

He added a cryptic warning: "Remember, that tomorrow you may be next."

When the ceremony concluded, the crowd shuffled from their seats as "God Bless America" was blared through woodwind and brass from the overhead balcony by members of the Conemaugh Valley School District high school band. O'Kicki, after nearly two decades in wait, would preside over the county courthouse. The directives he received from the Supreme Court of Pennsylvania that day were commissioned at his request. O'Kicki had asked the high court's administrators to examine Cambria County. What they found was a need to clean up severe backlogs. They questioned whether defendants were being tried within 180 days of being charged, in accordance with state law. They also wondered why civil cases from victims' families of the 1977 Johnstown Flood were still unresolved eleven years later.

"We will give this report very careful attention and follow its recommendations and discuss these points with fellow judges," O'Kicki said, "and we will bring about the solutions that the Supreme Court seeks."

In addition to calling for the Administrative Office of Pennsylvania Courts study, O'Kicki was considering other shakeups. He had employees inquiring about anomalies in the county's Domestic Relations Office, which was led by the judge who had been seated to his right during the ceremonies. Friends and associates would later say he was planning to empanel a countywide investigating grand jury to root out suspected corruption in the courthouse.

Simmering beneath the pomp and circumstance of the celebration, unbeknownst to the general public, was a silent battle of forces. The new president judge had learned just days earlier that he was the target of a Pennsylvania State Police probe into his official and personal affairs. Within a year, he'd be indicted by the Sixth Statewide Investigating Grand Jury, accused of frequenting brothels, assisting organized crime and demanding kickbacks in exchange for favorable rulings.

Within five years, O'Kicki would find himself an international fugitive desperately attempting to barter with the U.S. attorney general for leniency in exchange for information about links between the mob and big business in Johnstown.

PART I

"MY NAME IS 'JUDGE'"

Chapter 1

YOUTHFUL AMBITION

Cambria County president judge Norman A. Krumenacker III occupies a position that's perceived differently than it was just a few decades ago.

Gone is the blue shag carpeting on the walls designed, supposedly, to insulate a judge's office from "bugs" and inquisitive ears. The tales of shots fired at courthouse windows have faded to legend or, depending on who you ask, myth. And a hovering cloud of suspicion, innuendo and scandal has largely dissipated with the passing of the decades.

All of these facets were products in part of Judge Joseph F. O'Kicki, a predecessor and former friend to Krumenacker.

"I knew Joe O'Kicki from the time I was born," Krumenacker said during a 2019 interview in his office. "The reason being was—and I can't give you the year, this was so long ago—my father was the city solicitor in the early '60s and gave Joe O'Kicki and another attorney…jobs, like per diem–type work, for the City [of Johnstown] when they were researching properties for the redevelopment authority."

O'Kicki later returned the favor by bringing Krumenacker in as a young law clerk.

"One of the most brilliant men I've ever met in my life," Krumenacker said, "but he was at the edge. And I do believe over time, and I'm no MD, that he had a nervous breakdown that was never diagnosed."

Long before O'Kicki's life went under real or imagined assault by outlaw bikers—and later "the pigs, Arabs and Italians"—he lived a life like many other young immigrants in western Pennsylvania and across Appalachia.

Cambria County president judge Norman A. Krumenacker III shares his recollections of the late Joe O'Kicki. *Photo by Eric Kieta/*Daily American.

In his book *Johnstown Industry*, author Joshua M. Penrod recounts Cambria County's transformation from a sleepy agrarian outpost to a major industrial center. The area was settled by a man named Joseph Schantz in 1800. It was originally named Conemaugh Town but was renamed Johnstown in Schantz's honor in 1835.

By 1876, the nation's centennial, businesses such as Cambria Iron Co. had propelled the city to emergence as a major economic center. Cambria Iron Co. alone supplied 10 percent of America's iron rails, and the company employed more than four thousand people in a city of just ten thousand.

There were notable setbacks, such as the infamous Johnstown Flood of 1889—a horrific and largely preventable tragedy in which more than two thousand people lost their lives—but the city as a whole rebounded with regularity up through the mid-twentieth century. Johnstown's population and employment opportunities peaked in the 1920s.

The opportunities afforded by the expanding iron and steel industries during this era drew thousands of immigrants. Joseph O'Kicki's father, the senior, was among hundreds of thousands of Slovenes living under the Austrian Empire who left Europe for the United States around the turn of the twentieth century. He found work at the mill and later married Antonia Mary Martincik, who was sixteen years younger. Pennsylvania Department of Health records list Austria as the birthplace for both of them, and the couple's ties to present-day Slovenia would later haunt Pennsylvania State Police investigators.

The O'Kickis had a daughter, Olga, born on September 29, 1927. She died less than four months later on January 10, 1928. The cause listed on her death certificate is "convulsions…undetermined."

On the anniversary of Olga's death a year later, Antonia gave birth to Ladislava. She, like her sister, lived only a few months. Her grave states her date of death as May 27, 1929.

The following year, the couple welcomed a son to the world. Joseph F. O'Kicki Jr. was born on August 19, 1930.

In interviews with the *Times-Leader* and, much later, the *Philadelphia Inquirer*, O'Kicki discussed his upbringing at length. He said his father came to America from central Europe in 1902 at the age of sixteen to establish roots in Franklin Borough. Cambria Steel Co. had built the nearby Franklin Works facilities to help keep pace with both national and international demand for steel. The site began with sixty coke ovens and later added two hundred more. This massive operation became a burgeoning component of the economy in Johnstown, which saw its population peak at nearly sixty thousand in the 1920s. The men, women and even children of Cambria County mined the coal, stoked the furnaces and produced the iron and steel that built the nation's railroad system in times of peace and fed the war machine in times of conflict.

Though the senior O'Kicki worked in the Johnstown mills, his son said his primary talent was in stonemasonry. He believed that his father's skills were underappreciated. "I am ashamed to say that my father never made more than $2,800 in any year," O'Kicki once told a reporter.

The judge described his family as "rag poor," and perhaps for good reason. He said his father's lung collapsed in 1941 from silicosis. His mother found employment as a janitor as result. Soon, however, she also became ill. This

According to Pennsylvania Supreme Court justice John Flaherty, the storied Roxbury Bandshell in Johnstown was built with the assistance of Judge O'Kicki's father. The site remains a popular venue for summer concerts. *Photo by Bruce Siwy.*

forced O'Kicki, the lone able body in the household, into work at the young age of eleven. He scrubbed bathroom floors for a time and at the age of fourteen went into coal mining, digging both after school and on weekends.

George Fattman, a former editor of the *Johnstown Tribune-Democrat* newspaper and former news director at the local WJAC-TV news station, came to know O'Kicki as he rose from a little-known attorney to a prominent public figure after his unsuccessful run for U.S. Congress in 1970 and successful run for judge in 1971. He described O'Kicki as both intelligent and more than a little combative—a trait that might be attributed in part to his hardscrabble background and where he grew up.

"He intensely disliked the *Tribune-Democrat,* and that never went away," Fattman said. "I never found out why he intensely disliked the *Tribune-Democrat,* but I think it was part of his personality and the personality of a lot of ethnic people in Johnstown.

"[They believed] there was kind of this power structure, you know, the northern Europeans, I guess, who looked down their noses at these poor people of Slavic background and so forth. And I sensed that all over Johnstown. O'Kicki was kind of the epitome of that. You could tell that he felt put down, even though he was a brilliant man."

Perceived prejudice against central and eastern Europeans in Cambria County seemed to have given O'Kicki a chip on his shoulder. He might have used that as motivation to outdo his peers and elevate his social status.

Upon graduation from Franklin High School, top-of-his-class O'Kicki was unable to afford college. He found work as a photoengraver and overnight editor at the Tribune Publishing Co. in Johnstown before joining thousands of other locals in the ranks of the Bethlehem Steel behemoth at the age of twenty. An AFL-CIO scholarship later enabled him to attend the University of Pittsburgh at Johnstown, where he majored in physical chemistry.

According to O'Kicki, a highlight of his collegiate years came at the expense of U.S. representative John P. Saylor, a Republican representing the Twenty-Second Congressional District. O'Kicki was president of the student body and, as such, had the honor of calling on students to question the congressman. He said he deliberately chose students who had served in Korea. When some of them questioned the war efforts, Saylor—having no idea that they were former military—suggested they were cowards for not serving their country.

"Retribution was swift and fast," O'Kicki said. Saylor was booed off the stage but would have his revenge years later when he and O'Kicki went toe-to-toe in politics.

A recent look at Bon Air Street in Franklin Borough. Joe O'Kicki's parents lived along this road in the 1920s. *Photo by Bruce Siwy.*

After earning his bachelor's in physical chemistry, O'Kicki applied to the University of Pittsburgh Law School. But he said he was prohibited from attending because the Cambria County Bar Association told the school he was a communist. O'Kicki believed he'd been discriminated against because he could speak some Slovenian and Russian, because he'd opposed the war and because he was an "ethnic."

So O'Kicki reapplied for the U.S. Navy. He'd been barred from service eleven previous times because of back injuries he had suffered in a car accident. The twelfth time was the charm: his deferment was lifted, enabling him to serve full time from 1952 to 1954. He said he was able to shake off the "commie" label by appealing to Pitt in his U.S. Navy uniform.

In 1957, O'Kicki graduated with his law degree and returned to Cambria County. He was given his first job in the legal field by Andrew Gleason, patriarch of a Republican political dynasty in Pennsylvania, and married the former Theresa Caroff. He and Theresa eventually had seven children together, all of them girls.

Just as O'Kicki was starting his own family, he lost his father. The senior O'Kicki died in 1960.

J. F. O'KICKI

Left: A young Joseph O'Kicki appears in the 1957 yearbook for the University of Pittsburgh School of Law. *Courtesy of Tim Burns.*

Below: Joseph O'Kicki, his first wife, Theresa, and their seven daughters pose for a family photo. *Author's collection.*

The stonemason's son, however, was building quite a life for himself. O'Kicki opened his own law office in Johnstown and was admitted to the federal bar in 1963. He joined the state firemen's association and provided legal counsel to several local departments. For several years he worked as an attorney, serving as an assistant solicitor for Cambria County and earning money on the side teaching inorganic chemistry at Pitt-Johnstown and physics at St. Francis University in Loretto.

Brian Sukenik, whose parents were family friends with the O'Kicki family, was one of his students at Pitt-Johnstown. He remembered him as humorous and friendly, noting that O'Kicki sometimes invited him and other classmates out to eat after lessons. Often, he said, they were accompanied by Sheriff Joe Cavanaugh.

"[O'Kicki] said…he could go into any bar in Cambria County and have the owner give a free pitcher of beer," Sukenik said.

"Pizza was our choice of food. Wings didn't exist yet. [We ate] fish sandwiches too."

Even then, Sukenik said, he could sense some apprehension about O'Kicki.

"I think it was his way of protecting himself, by always having friends around, so no one tried anything. We never had any incidents. We went out to a different place every time we [went] out," he said.

In his private law practice, O'Kicki assisted clients with a variety of problems, including a particular landlord-tenant dispute that made a lasting impression on him.

"In 1967 a couple came to [my] law office and sought my legal help. They brought pictures of the premises where they lived and some of the people who were frequently around the place," O'Kicki wrote.

The husband and wife complained about the activities taking place primarily on weekends in the third floor apartment above them at 123 Fairfield Avenue in the [Morrellville] section of Johnstown. Either the W.E. Schonek insurance agency was on the first floor or else a Pa. Liquor store.

From the pictures I recognized several city policemen serving as doormen or guards at the staircase leading to the third floor. On the third floor was a private hotel, known as Penn Sota, a coporation solely owned by W.E. ("Wid") Schonek. From the observations of the clients, this hotel was used to entertain public officials and officials of Bethlehem Steel Corporation, where Schonek did a lot of supply business. Young pretty women appeared in the pictures. They, I later learned from my police sources, were recruited from surrounding counties and were usually nurses or school teachers. Because of the partying mostly on Fridays, Saturdays and Sundays, the couple and their children were continually disturbed from the noise above. They went to the police station to complain and stopped when they recognized the police officers as the same ones who [worked as doormen].…*One picture, to my shock, showed a sergeant of city detectives standing as guard to the third floor entrance. The clients reported this man frequently escorted ladies to the third floor.*

The noise complaint—allegedly stemming from a debauched confluence of sex appeal, corporate power, politicians, police protection and, he'd later assert, Mafia sanction—led O'Kicki to write and send a letter to Schonek, the millionaire owner of several area businesses. He informed Schonek that these tenants demanded a termination of their year-to-year lease and the return of their rent payments since they couldn't have "peaceful enjoyment" of their apartment. Schonek's attorney, former state senator Richard Green, replied that the contents of the letter were false. He threatened legal action against O'Kicki if he and his clients didn't "stop this malicious gossip."

"My only reply was to hand him several pictures and I explained that we had duplicates and were prepared to make proper distribution of them," O'Kicki said. "Within two hours Green came back to my office accepting my demands and a written settlement proposal."

"I submitted the same to my clients on the next day and they were ecstatic. They had gone to three other lawyers who advised that they had no legal rights."

This, according to O'Kicki, was his first brush with Schonek. The ambitious young attorney's subsequent forays into politics promised that it would not be his last.

In 1970, at the age of forty, O'Kicki became a Democratic challenger for Saylor's seat in Congress, one that he'd held since 1949. Saylor was known as a staunch conservationist who earned a 1970 award from the Izaak Walton League of America for "two decades of unprecedented leadership in the Congress of the United States for sound resource management, the preservation of natural scenic and cultural values, the maintenance of a quality environment and the unalienable right of citizens to be involved in resources and environmental decisions."

Candidate O'Kicki mocked his opponent for his environment concerns. "When John P. Saylor took office in 1949, the dollar was a lot bigger and went a lot further," he wrote on one campaign flier. "Today—after you paid

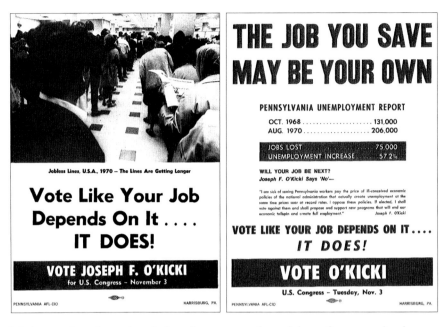

Left: A campaign ad prominently featuring a commonly used slogan for congressional candidate Joseph O'Kicki: "Vote Like Your Job Depends On It…IT DOES!" *Courtesy of Sylvia Onusic.*

Right: Joseph O'Kicki sought to make the economy a primary issue while challenging U.S. representative John P. Saylor in the 1970 election. *Courtesy of Sylvia Onusic.*

him nearly 500,000 of your tax dollars, the records show that he's more interested in his bills to help penguins and sea lions than in your bills. You're being short-changed."

Unemployment and inflation, according to O'Kicki, were the most important concerns of Saylor's constituents in the commonwealth. He attacked Saylor for his economic record.

"I am sick of seeing Pennsylvania workers pay the price of ill-conceived economic policies of the national administration that actually create unemployment at the same time prices soar at record rates," O'Kicki wrote in a 1970 campaign flyer stating that Pennsylvania had lost seventy-five thousand jobs between 1968 and 1970. This poster and others included the AFL-CIO acronym for the Pennsylvania American Federation of Labor and Congress of Industrial Organizations, the largest organization of trade unions in the United States. "I oppose these policies. If elected, I shall vote against them and shall propose and support new programs that will end our economic tailspin and create full employment."

He concluded the campaign ad with: "Vote Like Your Job Depends On It...IT DOES!"

On another flyer, O'Kicki wrote:

The Federal Government takes: Income tax from your wages; Social Security tax from your wages; Unemployment Compensation tax from your wages; Seven cents per gallon of gasoline tax; excise tax on cigarettes, liquor, beer and wine; tax on your air travel; tax on your automobile tires and accessories; tax on your fire arms and fishing equipment; tax on sugar; tax on your property and money that you leave to your children; tax on gifts that you make to your grandchildren; and tax on your phone conversations to your children and friends.

Elect a new man who is pledged to tax reform.

This venture into politics was ultimately unsuccessful. Saylor fended off O'Kicki's bid for Congress by a narrow margin, edging him out by just 725 votes. Saylor would die of a heart attack in Houston, Texas, just three years later. He was succeeded by John "Jack" Murtha, a Democrat who would become chairman of the influential House of Representatives defense appropriations subcommittee during his remarkable thirty-six-year tenure in office.

O'Kicki was undeterred by his 1970 election loss. He made a bid for the ballot again a year later, this time seeking to become a judge in the Cambria County Court of Common Pleas. This experience may have contributed to his dislike of the local daily paper, which was co-owned by his general election opponent. O'Kicki wrote:

It was my good fortune to win the Democratic nomination for judge, defeating a popular District Attorney. On the night of the primary election, Len Laporta and I were camped out in my law office receiving the election results as they came to the courthouse. It wasn't until 5 a.m. that I was assured of victory. About 6 a.m. Bill Santoro, a radio newscaster, came into my office and congratulated me. He brought with [him] Wid Schonek, whom I had not previously met or recognized...and Wid congratulated me.

Wid never put one cent of money directly or indirectly into my election campaign. My Republican opponent in the fall election was James E. Mayer, part owner of the only daily newspaper, the Tribune-Democrat, *and whose brother Richard managed it. I later learned that Schonek quietly supported Mayer because he, Schonek, didn't want to offend the* Tribune.

According to O'Kicki, encounters with Schonek were sparse and sporadic for his first decade on the bench. He noted, however, that Schonek and other local powerbrokers would lean on the judges and other Cambria County officials to hire friends and family.

"Along with Democratic County chairman John Torquato and Republican Boss, Andrew W. Gleason, Schonek made recommendations to me for the hiring of various people whenever vacancies occurred. Schonek controlled two of the three county commissioners who hire and set salaries for all courthouse personnel except the judges," O'Kicki said.

As he was twice nominated for the Federal Bench, O'Kicki's intelligence was widely recognized within the judicial community. But there were other facets to his reputation. Journalist Carol Morello of Knight-Ridder Services remarked on the eccentricity that became the judge's hallmark at the Ebensburg courthouse in a 1989 report published by the *Edmonton Journal*:

> *During O'Kicki's 17 years as a judge, controversy was a constant companion. He was known for his unconventional decisions, such as the time he jailed all nine members of the Penn Cambria School Board in 1985 when he thought they ignored his order to keep school open throughout June....Lawyers complain that O'Kicki periodically insisted they make*

A street-side view of the Cambria County Courthouse in Ebensburg. *Photo by Bruce Siwy.*

appointments with him three or four weeks in advance, yet he kept lawyers and juries waiting to begin trials while he called in attorneys to chat about the weather or football.

As president-elect of the Pennsylvania Conference of Trial Court Judges, O'Kicki in 1983 announced his resignation from the Pennsylvania Bar Association after the organization rated Allegheny County judge Nicholas Papadakos and Berks County judge Thomas J. Eshelman, both of the Common Pleas Court, as "not qualified" to serve on the Supreme Court of Pennsylvania.

Though O'Kicki himself had been rated "well qualified" by the state bar, he characterized the low ratings of Papadakos and Eshelman as "ludicrous...an insult to voters." He accused the bar association—made up of approximately a dozen lawyers and judges and three non-lawyer members—of becoming a subjective and politically motivated group. The bar declined to respond to O'Kicki's resignation and comments.

While these anecdotes are noteworthy aspects of his tenure practicing law and on the bench in Cambria County, perhaps the most remarkable incident prior to his short tenure as president judge occurred in the aftermath of a violent clash between a biker gang and police officers in 1980.

The Outlaws trial was intense and traumatic and was haunted years later by chilling murder-for-hire allegations—not against the bikers, but against O'Kicki.

Chapter 2

OUTLAWS AND OTHER ENEMIES

Mundys Corner, an unincorporated Cambria County community about six miles west of the courthouse in Ebensburg, was once home to the Snack Shack. This tiny roadside tavern was popular with the Outlaws, a biker gang with a nationwide presence and a heavy reputation.

Just before midnight on July 7, 1980, violence cut through the boozy haze of the establishment. A barroom-brawl-turned-shootout erupted between Outlaws bikers and three strangers they may have mistaken for members of the Pagans, a rival gang. The truth, however, was that these three men were non-uniformed Pennsylvania State Police officers.

Who was to blame for what transpired that night can evoke strong conflicting opinions, even to this day. So what follows is the account that was accepted by a jury.

According to courtroom reporting by the *Altoona Mirror* newspaper, the Outlaws became convinced that the plainclothes police were Pagans. One of the Outlaws decided to hit Officer Clifford Jobe Jr. with a baseball bat. Another struck Officer Brian Craig with a club. Outlaw Scott Fetzer of Ebensburg then dragged Jobe outside while holding the nose of a .38-caliber derringer to the officer's head while fellow Outlaw David Graves told Fetzer to kill the man.

Fearing for his life, Jobe grabbed a gun from his boot and rolled behind a car. He identified himself as a police officer and fired two shots at the Snack Shack. Jobe also yelled for fellow officer William T. Matis, who was outside

A black-and-white shot of the Snack Shack, a roadside tavern favored by members of the Outlaws biker gang in the 1970s and '80s. *Courtesy of the "Jackson-Township historical preservation" Facebook page.*

when the fight began, to go in and call for backup. When Matis stepped into the bar, Snack Shack bartender and Outlaw member Nicholas Kush fired a shotgun blast into the officer's stomach.

Outside the establishment, Jobe arrested Outlaws Fetzer, Kenneth Swope of Johnstown and Philip Brosch of Revloc as they tried to drag a nearly unconscious Craig outside. Both Craig and Matis survived the ordeal but suffered permanent injuries. Fetzer, Graves, Kush, Brosch and Swope, as well as Dennis Anderson of Ebensburg and Michael Szekeresh of Nanty Glo, were slapped with dozens of charges.

The police testified that they were undercover at the Snack Shack to investigate the club for drug dealing. Cambria County district attorney Gerald Long said the Outlaws made "unprovoked, planned, sudden and cowardly" attacks on the officers.

Defense attorneys Daniel Lovette and Louis LaLumere, meanwhile, argued that Craig started the fight by hitting Anderson, one of the Outlaws. They said Szekeresh and Kush only clubbed the officers in an attempt to rescue Anderson. None of the Outlaws confessed to shooting Matis.

In the end, the jury sided with police and prosecution. The seven Outlaws were convicted on thirty-eight total charges and imprisoned at the jail in Cambria County. Their sentences were, in most cases, the maximum, ranging from seven to forty years. Members of the gang expressed disbelief upon hearing the severity of their punishment.

Judge Joseph O'Kicki presided over the trial for members of this biker gang. He'd tell friends and colleagues that he feared for his life, that the Outlaws vowed vengeance for their lengthy prison terms. It wasn't the first or last time the judge would claim he'd made dangerous enemies.

According to Cambria County judge Norman A. Krumenacker III, the Outlaws affair was among several significant stressors in O'Kicki's life.

"During the trial—and this goes to his paranoia…he [had] the parking lot cleared out here at the side and had the helicopter here," Krumenacker said. "It just got to the level of security that was over the top.

"His [behavior] was real bizarre."

George Fattman recalled a particularly odd encounter with O'Kicki. The judge showed up one day at the *Tribune-Democrat* office, distraught over news coverage of some sort.

"He just leaned over toward me and he put his hands on my desk and he said, 'I just want you to know, you don't hold all the cards,'" Fattman said.

"I'm not quite sure what that meant, but it was the way he dealt with people. You know he could be intimidating, and you had to…stand up to him."

The judge often made a point to talk about the animosity between the Outlaws and himself. Fattman said O'Kicki once told him that the bikers made an attempt on his life.

> *One day when we were supposed to have lunch,* [I] *went to the courthouse and he invited me into his office…off the chamber and had these windows behind his desk, behind his head. So he said, "Look at those bulletholes— those were shots from the Outlaws at my windows." And he said, "It's so bad that before I go home at night I check with the state police and they tell me which route I should take to get home." His home was in Richland Township.*
>
> *So I don't know how long that went on.* [State police] *may have watched out for him because he was in a dangerous position vis a vis the Outlaw gang. But it was interesting that he called me up to point that out to me.*

The allegations went both ways.

Anderson, who was among the Outlaws convicted in 1981, later told authorities that O'Kicki spoke with him privately on two occasions while he served his ten-year sentence. He said one of the meetings took place in the judge's office and the other in the warden's office of the old county jail. According to Anderson, O'Kicki indicated that he was willing to help the Outlaws secure an early release from jail in exchange for cash and a few favors.

O'Kicki, Anderson said, asked for $25,000 from each of the seven bikers convicted in the assault, a .22-caliber gun with a silencer—and a contract for them to kill his wife, Theresa.

<hr />

THE DECADES HAVE NOT dulled Sylvia Onusic's sense of outrage for her husband. Nor have they prompted her to purge her home of his files.

During a 2019 interview from her residence, the second former Mrs. Joseph F. O'Kicki pulled out boxes of yellow notepads once used by the judge's secretary to take his messages and keep his appointments. She shared faxes, letters, lawsuits, news clippings and VHS tapes of television coverage. Her piercing eyes sparkled with exuberance as she recounted her first real conversation with the judge.

Onusic met O'Kicki when he was teaching at the University of Pittsburgh at Johnstown. She said she was working at Mercy Hospital in Johnstown in the early 1980s when she decided to continue her education. Because she needed some general education credits before enrolling in grad school, she

Sylvia Onusic, Joe O'Kicki's second wife, photographed during a 2019 interview in her home. *Photo by Eric Kieta/*Daily American.

signed up for classes at Pitt-Johnstown. It was on this campus that she first met the judge, who was one of her instructors there.

"I always thought O'Kicki was an Irish name," Onusic said.

"It was St. Patrick's Day.…He was out in the hall talking to some students, and I went up to him and said, 'Oh, happy St. Patrick's Day, judge.' And he took notice of me and he said, 'Oh, thank you, but I'm not Irish, I'm Slovenian.' I said, 'Oh, ha, I'm Slovenian.' So then we talked in the hall… [and] it progressed from there."

Onusic—the former Sylvia Notich and Sylvia Duke—married the judge when he divorced his first wife, Theresa, in 1986. The notion that her husband was fearful of retaliation from the Outlaws was not unfamiliar to her. She recalled a story he told her about having Tony Trigona, one of his tipstaff county employees, serve as something of a security guard. She said:

> [They] had set up a little headquarters on his property. I don't know how that happened, but just to watch over cars coming. It was a very long driveway, and somebody could come up the driveway and stop at one point where there was like an office swimming pool building. And they could have gotten out and done anything, I mean, because it was a big piece of property, that O'Kicki property.
>
> He told me a couple times a helicopter came and picked him up. And he also told me the story—I'm not sure, but I do have a news clipping—that one of his daughter's roommates was murdered and he thought it had to do with the Outlaws.…I didn't know if I really would believe that or not because I never talked to the daughters, but he had that clipping in a file, which meant to me there was something to it. Why would he keep that?…Yeah, he was concerned for his kids. He was really worried for his kids.

The Trigona name has special relevance in this story. His disgust with the judge—indirectly, over Onusic—provided a significant link in the chain of events that ultimately brought infamy to the O'Kicki name.

To whom it may concern: this is to inform you as of Sept. 12, 1983 I have accepted a position of employment with an out-of-state firm.

Therefore please remove my name from the county payroll as of the above date. I wish to thank the commissioners and the employees at the Cambria County Courthouse for the courtesy and kindness they extended to me during my employment there. If I have any vacation time due me and also my retirement fund, please have it forwarded to my home address. Also if there is any way I can keep my Blue Cross and Blue Shield and pay for it myself, please let me know. Yours truly, Anthony S. Trigona.

The resignation letter was dated September 24, 1983. Trigona was expressing his decision to move on from his tipstaff position working for Cambria County and, more specifically, O'Kicki.

Years later, Trigona recounted his history with the judge and his family. He wrote in a letter that they met during a home improvement show held at the Cambria County War Memorial Arena in the 1970s. At the time, he was operating a small business called A.S. Trigona & Sons. He sold the O'Kickis a kitchen for their new home that day and later renovated their bathrooms as well.

A few years later, A.S. Trigona & Sons was in trouble. The 1977 Johnstown Flood extinguished lives, leveled homes and crippled the local economy. It was the beginning of the end for the city's once-robust steel industry and for Trigona's business as well. He filed for Chapter 11 bankruptcy in Pittsburgh during December 1979.

According to Trigona, O'Kicki learned of his financial troubles and offered him a tipstaff job at the courthouse in 1981. This began on a per diem basis and then evolved to full time. He indicated that his time with the judge and his first wife, Theresa, resulted in a strong bond with both Mr. and Mrs. O'Kicki.

But a month before his resignation, Trigona wrote, O'Kicki asked him to help move a bed from his home. When he arrived, he found that Theresa was crying. These marital problems were apparently news to Trigona. He said that the disintegration of the O'Kicki marriage bothered him because of his friendship with both of them.

The falling out between Trigona and O'Kicki in 1983 had long-term ramifications for the judge because, five years later, Trigona would be granted an order of immunity from Judge Levy Anderson to provide testimony against O'Kicki for the Sixth Statewide Investigating Grand Jury.

IN THE COURT OF COMMON PLEAS

OF PHILADELPHIA COUNTY, PENNSYLVANIA

IN RE: The Sixth Statewide   : Supreme Court of Pennsylvania
                                   : 189 E.D. Misc. Dkt. 1987
Investigating Grand Jury   :
                                   : Philadelphia County Common Pleas
                                   : Misc. Motion No. 88-00-1409

ORDER OF IMMUNITY

ANTHONY TRIGONA:

It is the Order of this Court, as Supervising Judge of the Sixth Statewide Investigating Grand Jury, in accordance with the provisions of the Act of October 4, 1978, P.L. 873, No. 168, 42 Pa.C.S.A. Section 5947, that you shall not be excused from testifying on the ground that the testimony or evidence required of you may tend to incriminate you or subject you to a penalty or forfeiture.

However, no testimony or other information compelled under this Order, or any information directly or indirectly derived from such testimony or other information, may be used against you in a criminal action, except a prosecution for perjury, giving a false statement, contempt, or otherwise failing to comply with this Order, or, as evidence, where otherwise admissible, in any proceeding where you are not a criminal defendant.

An Order of Immunity issued by the supervising judge of the Sixth Statewide Investigating Grand Jury for Tony Trigona of the Johnstown area. Trigona was among several former staffers of Judge O'Kicki who provided testimony against him. *Photo by Eric Kieta/Daily American.*

—————————

TROOPER WALT KOMOROSKI REPRESENTED one-half of the investigative team tasked with looking at Cambria County corruption as O'Kicki prepared his ascent to president judge.

Now retired and clean-shaven from crown to chin, Komoroski recalled being partnered with Corporal Bill Russell for the job in April 1988.

Komoroski was a member of the Pennsylvania State Police's white-collar crime unit, while Russell represented the vice unit.

Komoroski said the genesis of the O'Kicki investigation took root when his new supervisor called for a meeting about illegal gambling in the area. He said:

> *Troop A Vice members, and there were two or three of them at the meeting, complained that it seemed like every time we began an operation...in the mountains, word got out so quickly that they were unsuccessful. And by investigation I'm talking about a covert undercover operation that nine times out of ten involved electronic surveillance. And by electronic surveillance, I mean phone taps, wire taps, that sort of thing, and standard visual observation and surveillance techniques.*
>
> *Of course* [the supervisor] *wanted to know, "Well, what's the problem up there? Why aren't you successful? Why is this information getting out?" And there were some allegations of political corruption. And he wanted—he demanded—to know, "Who's politically corrupt? What's going on up there?"*

According to Komoroski, Troop A vice officers noted that a judge's signature was needed for the search warrants involved with some of these surveillance operations. This led to speculation that one or more members of the Cambria County judiciary were tipping off the people who ran illegal gambling in the region.

"The next question was, 'Well, if there's someone that's dirty up there, we should investigate them,'" Komoroski said. "'Who are we talking about?' There were various names tossed around at the magistrate level and at the criminal court level. And one of the names that was tossed out at the time was Judge O'Kicki."

A prosecutor would later estimate that approximately 553 interviews were conducted during the course of the probe. Komoroski said he and Russell used a variety of methods to build their case.

"When you have an allegation [against someone] like this particular fellow, you say to yourself, 'Now, how do I prove that? How do I prove that happened?' It's word against his word. It's a 'he-said, he-said' situation. Well, the only thing you can do is to try to capture conversion, okay. [But] we were unsuccessful," Komoroski said.

"We had wired this fellow up. We got court approval to do that. We were observing a confrontation that occurred outside the courthouse from a

Walt Komoroski, a retired white-collar crime investigator for the Pennsylvania State Police, poses for a picture at the *Daily American* newspaper office in Somerset. *Photo by Eric Kieta/*Daily American.

van. And [O'Kicki] almost said the magic words. But he finally said, 'Get away from me, old man' and walked away."

Komoroski remembered feeling intense pressure during this investigation. This came not only from supervisors but also from sources. Those cooperating with police were apprehensive about feeling O'Kicki's wrath if he was not successfully prosecuted.

"If you're going to throw arrows at the king," Komoroski said with a smile, "make sure you kill the king."

It wasn't, however, the only politically significant investigation taking place at the Cambria County Courthouse at this time.

O'Kicki had commissioned a probe of his own around this same time, possibly even before state police began prying into his personal affairs.

Chapter 3

DUELING INVESTIGATIONS

Cambria County native Brian Sukenik said he was in Las Vegas for a trade show in the spring of 1988 when the meeting took place. He recalled walking cross-town from Union Plaza to the Vegas Hilton for what he believed would be a social call with an old family friend who once taught him at the University of Pittsburgh at Johnstown.

Greeting him at the hotel, he said, was his pal Joe O'Kicki. They went up to the judge's hotel room and said hi to O'Kicki's wife, mother-in-law and newborn son. Then O'Kicki ushered him to a far corner of the suite.

According to Sukenik, O'Kicki was asking him to reconsider employment with the county. For four years in the early 1980s, Sukenik had worked as a hearings officer in Cambria County's domestic relations office. In 1984, he started raising questions about expense accounts recorded by the office's middle management personnel. He looked namely at travel expense reimbursements for employees on sick days; excessive mileage claims and travel expenses for trips not made; and additional record alterations. County commissioners, Sukenik later said in a civil suit, fired him for his troubles as retaliation for looking into records he believed had been falsified for the benefit of select courthouse personnel.

In Vegas, O'Kicki told Sukenik he was weeks away from becoming president judge of Cambria County. He wanted Sukenik to leave his job and return to Pennsylvania to help him investigate whether criminal activity was indeed taking place in the domestic relations office for a countywide investigating grand jury he planned to empanel.

A still frame of Cambria County employee Brian Sukenik, who visited the 814 Worx building along Main Street in Johnstown to explain his role in rooting out irregularities in government accounting. *Photo by Eric Kieta/*Daily American.

Unassuming and bespectacled beneath his blood-red "KEEP AMERICA GREAT" hat, Sukenik recounted the judge's request. "It was getting the documentation, which was hard to do. Unless you're on the inside, you don't have access to it all," he said. "It was just rumor at that time. But then later on, when I came back as deputy court administrator, that's one of the first things I looked at was the expense accounts and the computer invoices. And that's where all the questions were being raised."

O'Kicki had an undated, unsigned three-page memo that appeared to be drafted by county employees. It stated: "We are submitting the enclosed data with a fervent request that you conduct an investigation in the Domestic Relations Office. It is strongly urged that for complete verification of the following allegations that ALL records be subpeoned [*sic*], those kept in-house such as daily recording keeping books versus records sunmitted [*sic*] to Personnel and other departments."

Among the allegations was the idea that—as Sukenik had suspected in 1984—supervisors of the office were submitting false time sheets for themselves and others. Another was that the domestic relations office routinely hired friends and family of supervisors without filling those positions when those individuals left the county. This was evidence, according to the whistleblowers, that spending on these roles had been unnecessary and used primarily for the incestuous benefit of supervisors.

"In fairness to the employees of the DRO who do not receive extra days off or sick days taken but not properly marked, we feel strongly that abuses of these natures should not be tolerated or be permitted to continue, nor should they be ignored," the anonymous county workers wrote. "Not only are we concered [*sic*] with the support victims where it is obvious the particular defendants are being given extreme leniencies, we are concerned of what is happening at our work place. We know you will be taking over at President Judge in May and hope you will look into these matters."

The whistleblowers went even further. Their most serious charge raised questions about county contracts with an outside entity: "A $25,000 feasibility study by Ecco—the company awarded the bid for office computer/word processing system. The $25,000 was paid in two installments, the last one via

Dear Judge O'Kicki:

We are submitting the enclosed data with a fervent request that you conduct
an investigation in the Domestic Relations Office.
It is strongly urged that for complete verification of the following allegations
that ALL records be subpeoned, those kept in-house such as daily record keeping
books versus records sunmitted to Personnel and other departments.

Allegations are as follows:

1. Abuse of time sheets:

    This area is being abused by three supervisors: Jacob T. St. Clair,
    Director, Kenneth F. Clark, Assistant Director and Lisa M. Sheredy,
    Case Management Supervisor. Not only are they, themselves, submitting
    false attendance information, but they are continously submitting
    altered time-sheets for certain employees with Domestic Relations.
    Jacob T. St. Clair - absent 72 day in 1987. 7 days alloted for
    conferences, 15 vacation days, 2 personal days - 48 total unexcused
    absences. The majority of these were used on Wednesdays or Fridays for
    the purpose of playing golf.

2. Particulars:

    (a) He was involved in an auto accident of which an account appeared
         in the Tribune Democrat. Date of accident 8-29-87.

    (b) He participated in a golf tournament and was among of group of
         winners televised on WJAC in June, 1987. These days he was marked
         on the time sheet as being at work.

    The time sheets they continue to alter accurate time off for these
    particular employees:

    (1) Lee Ann Batdorf - sister of Lisa Sheredy.

    (2) Lee Ann Yeckley - close friend of Lisa Sheredy.

    (3) Mona Soyka - Jacob St. Clair's secretary.

    (4) Tracy McCall - clerk.

EXHIBIT X-2 (i)

Portion of a three-page letter that Judge O'Kicki said he received in March 1988. The letter
outlines suspected corruption within the Cambria County Domestic Relations Office by
whistleblowers employed by this department. *Courtesy of Sylvia Onusic.*

Federal Express to enable Mr. Joe Ott of Ecco, to meet his payroll. No report ever relayed to the DRO on the result of this study."

County employees were suggesting that their superiors were siphoning off county tax dollars for phantom studies to an outside firm for unknown reasons. This rose above even the unapproved paid leave and nepotism, and though Sukenik was intrigued by the opportunity to finish what he started in 1984, he was already working at Mid-America Corp. in Frankfort, Kentucky. The company specialized in court, police and records management software, and its affiliated companies were later awarded a state courts automation contract in 1989–90 by the Pennsylvania Supreme Court. Sukenik considered it a solid job.

Ultimately, however, he went with his old family friend. Sukenik was formally rehired as a Cambria County employee in August 1988. His new title: deputy court administrator.

In just weeks, evidence of excessive and questionable payments to Ecco was submitted to several different authorities, first by O'Kicki himself on September 15, 1988, and a short time later by Sukenik.

"As our Chief Legal Counsel explained to you by phone, we are not the investigative arm of the Judiciary, and I therefore have referred the material to the Attorney General of the Commonwealth and the State Judicial Inquiry and Review Board," Nancy Sobolevitch, court administrator of Pennsylvania, wrote in response to Sukenik on October 27, 1988. "Any further information or materials should be forwarded to either or both."

Robert L. Keuch, executive director for the Commonwealth of Pennsylvania Judicial Inquiry and Review Board, wrote:

> *Since you are alleging possible criminal violations, we would, consistent with our standing policies, defer jurisdiction in this matter, at least initially, to the appropriate prosecutorial authorities. Therefore, I have taken the liberty of referring your letter and its enclosures to the Western Regional Office of the Attorney General since I am aware that that office has an inquiry ongoing into matters in the Cambria County Courts.*

The name Lawrence Claus is tellingly CCed on the letter from Keuch. Claus, who worked as deputy attorney general at the time, would become a prominent figure and well-recognized name amid the incoming political storm to Cambria County.

U.S. Department of Justice officials also issued a response. "Please be advised that this office is in receipt of your letter dated October 17, 1988,

COMMONWEALTH OF PENNSYLVANIA
PENNSYLVANIA STATE POLICE
1800 ELMERTON AVENUE
HARRISBURG, PA. 17110

COLONEL RONALD M. SHARPE
COMMISSIONER

October 26, 1988

Mr. Brian Sukenik
c/o Robert Sukenik
128 Kinzey Street
Johnstown, PA   15904

Dear Mr. Sukenik:

Thank you for your letter regarding the possible irregularities in the Cambria County Domestic Relations Office.

The Pennsylvania State Police are currently investigating the reported irregularities associated with the Computer System in the Cambria County Domestic Relations Office. We are attempting to ascertain if any Pennsylvania Criminal Code Statutes were violated.

Your letter contains substantially the same information received by our Bureau of Criminal Investigation in correspondence dated September 15, 1988 from the Honorable Judge Joseph F. O'Kicki, Cambria County Court.

I appreciate your concern in this matter. We may have occasion to contact you during the course of the investigation.

Sincerely,

Ronald M. Sharpe

Colonel Ronald M. Sharpe
Commissioner

Exhibit 7-A

A Pennsylvania State Police correspondence with Geistown resident Brian Sukenik confirming their receipt of records indicative of irregularities in the Cambria County Domestic Relations Office. *Courtesy of Sylvia Onusic.*

concerning possible irregularities in the Cambria County Domestic Relations Office Federal IV-D funding....Thank you for bringing these matters to our attention," J. Alan Johnson, United States attorney for the Western District of Pennsylvania, said in an October 21, 1988 letter to Sukenik.

State police, for their part, acknowledged opening an official probe into the Ecco payments. "The Pennsylvania State Police are currently investigating the reported irregularities associated with the Computer System in the Cambria County Domestic Relations Office," Colonel Ronald M. Sharpe wrote in response to Sukenik on October 26, 1988. "We are attempting to ascertain if any Pennsylvania Criminal Code Statutes were violated.

"I appreciate your concern in this matter. We may have occasion to contact you during the course of the investigation."

That occasion came in April 1989, when Sukenik said he was called by State Trooper Robert M. Ando.

But O'Kicki's countywide grand jury never materialized. State authorities beat him to the punch with a grand jury of their own.

On October 7, 1988—just four months after he became president judge of Cambria County—O'Kicki was asked to take a leave of absence or be suspended by the Pennsylvania Supreme Court's Judicial Inquiry and Review Board.

Within a week of O'Kicki's suspension, newly appointed president Judge Caram Abood moved to fire Sukenik. Cambria County Commissioners approved the dismissal on October 15, 1988. Other O'Kicki hires were terminated in April 1989.

The judge would soon face seventy-six charges. If convicted of just a fraction of these counts, the judge was looking at years in prison.

Chapter 4

THE PRESENTMENT

I n the months following Judge O'Kicki's appointment as president judge of Cambria County, locals heard rumors that he was under some sort of investigation. This became the talk of Johnstown after he was formally suspended.

Ebensburg attorney Tim Burns could vaguely recall aspects of the O'Kicki affair, even though he was in high school at the time of the scandal. Speculation swirled around the largely rural county as the commonwealth began to hit local residents with subpoenas to testify.

The judge was already well known in the county. Now he was headed to infamy.

"To be blunt, most people on the street if you ask them today—and this is no disrespect to our current judges—but most people [couldn't] name one judge. Thirty years ago, you say 'Judge O'Kicki' [and] everybody in Cambria County could say who Judge O'Kicki was," Burns said.

The state Supreme Court put an end to the speculation in October 1988 when the justices issued a unanimous order relieving O'Kicki of his administrative and judicial duties. A spokesman for the Administrative Office of the Pennsylvania Courts told the press that O'Kicki would continue to receive his $80,500 salary amid the suspension.

Allegations against the Cambria County president judge were sweeping and sensational. The grand jury report—called at that that time a "presentment"—was issued in March 1989. It recommended charging O'Kicki with official oppression, criminal conspiracy to commit bribery,

INTRODUCTION

We, the members of the Sixth Statewide Investigating Grand Jury, have received and reviewed testimonial and documentary evidence pertaining to allegations of public corruption and related criminal law violations in Cambria County, Pennsylvania. This investigation was conducted pursuant to Notice of Submission of Investigation Number 13 and, by this interim Presentment, this Grand Jury does hereby make the following findings of fact and recommendations.

FINDINGS AND RECOMMENDATIONS

Based on the evidence which has been presented before it, the Grand Jury finds that Joseph O'Kicki, Judge of the Court of Common Pleas of Cambria County, has engaged in a continuing practice of public corruption and misuse of his office for a considerable period of time. This case arose out of a joint investigative effort initiated by Pennsylvania State Police officers from Troop A, Greensburg, Vice Unit, and from the White Collar Crime Unit, Findlay Barracks. Throughout this inquiry, this Grand Jury heard testimony from numerous witnesses and examined a significant amount of documentary evidence that was brought before it. This evidence demonstrates that, at least since the late 1970's and into the 1980's, Judge O'Kicki has used his public office in order to enhance his own financial holdings.

Perhaps the most concise single piece of documentary evidence reflective of how Judge O'Kicki intermingled his

Page 1 of the grand jury presentment outlining the commonwealth's case against Judge O'Kicki. *Author's collection.*

demanding property to secure employment, violations of the Pennsylvania Ethics Act, bribery, criminal coercion, theft of services, obstructing the administration of law, misapplication of property of a government institution, theft by extortion, perjury, violations of the Pennsylvania Election Code, violations of the Pennsylvania Anti Bid–Rigging Act, violations of the Pennsylvania Insurance Act, false application for certificate of title or registration, execution of documents by deception, violations of the Pennsylvania Securities Act, felony criminal mischief and the illegal extension of a water line.

"Joseph O'Kicki, Judge of the Court of Common Pleas of Cambria County, has engaged in a continuing practice of public corruption and misuse of his office for a considerable period of time....At least since the late 1970's and into the 1980's, Judge O'Kicki has used his public office in order to enhance his own financial holdings," the presentment stated.

"O'Kicki's apparent belief [is] that in his official capacity he was justified in granting 'favors' to those who came before him concerning official matters."

Additionally, "the motive for Judge O'Kicki's improper and illegal conduct appears to be personal financial gain. However, it is also apparent that on some occasions when he took inappropriate action in his capacity as a Judge, O'Kicki himself may not have benefited monetarily."

The following is a summation of the grand jury allegations.

Betty Krisko and Brenda Nasser, both secretaries for O'Kicki, described their workplace as rife with sexual harassment and humiliation. Krisko said she was once called into his office to find him wearing "nothing but a pair of bikini-like briefs." On another occasion, she said, he did not appear to be wearing anything at all while sitting behind his desk.

Nasser testified that she once saw O'Kicki in his office wearing nothing but a pair of yellow jockey shorts.

"When Nasser failed to respond to the Judge in a positive way, she says O'Kicki became enraged and started to throw things until Nasser left and closed the door behind her," the presentment states. "Nasser also testified that Judge O'Kicki solicited her to have sex with him at her house prior to the two of them reporting for work. Nasser said that when she refused the Judge's suggestion, he began to treat her very badly. She subsequently left the Johnstown area and relocated out of state."

Nasser also said the judge never offered to reimburse her for gas even though she often drove him to work.

Female subordinates weren't the only ones who accused the judge of mistreatment.

George Koban worked for O'Kicki from July 1982 until September 1983. He testified that he had asked O'Kicki about securing a higher-paying job with the county during that time. The judge allegedly told Koban that he'd take care of this request if Koban gave him $500.

Some time later, when Koban asked the judge about the $500, O'Kicki reportedly told him, "I gave it to the [county] commissioners." Koban asked one of the commissioners about it, who denied receiving the money. O'Kicki called the commissioners "liars." When Koban asked the judge about the money on a second occasion, this time at a bar, O'Kicki became angry and called him an "unfaithful employee" for contacting the commissioners about the money.

Other county employees told investigators that they would haul firewood and stoke the wood burner for the judge's home while on the clock. Tipstaff Tony Trigona said O'Kicki once directed him to have his own vehicle "washed, waxed and full of gas." O'Kicki then took Trigona's car for a trip to his daughter's wedding in Chicago. The judge, according to Trigona, did not reimburse him for the use of his vehicle.

Another tipstaff said he picked up envelopes for the judge at Birk Transfer, a Parkhill trucking company, and collected his rent money for him on a regular basis.

O'Kicki's troubles were entwined with fellow members of the Cambria County legal community. Attorney Richard "Dick" Green—who purchased O'Kicki's law firm along with Caram Abood before Abood became a judge—testified that O'Kicki often entered his office, usually on Friday afternoons, to ask for "loans" of at least $500. The judge never offered to repay the money, Green said, noting that he sometimes "ducked out" in an effort to avoid the judge.

Additionally, Green accused the judge of extortion.

O'Kicki once ruled in favor of one of Green's clients with a "molded verdict" that increased the jury-mandated amount, adding "annoyance damages" that enhanced the total by $100,000. This brought the total awarded to Green's client to $240,000.

After the hearing, O'Kicki allegedly asked Green, "Don't you think I ought to get a commission…or part of your fee on this case?" Green said that he didn't pay the judge anything and that he didn't report the matter to the Commonwealth of Pennsylvania Judicial Inquiry and Review Board because he feared retaliation from O'Kicki.

Another count relayed that Judge Max Pavolich, a magistrate in southern Cambria County, bought an investment property in Beaverdale from O'Kicki and his first wife. When he later told O'Kicki he could no longer afford the bank payments, O'Kicki sent a letter to First United Federal stating that it would "behoove the bank to talk" with him about the Pavlovich loan. Bank officers agreed to forgive $15,000 of Pavlovich's remaining $18,000 balance.

A bank officer testified that O'Kicki was known to be "a pretty tough negotiator, someone who…you wouldn't want to cross."

O'Kicki was accused of bullying bank employees for personal benefit as well. In October 1984, the judge bought a car from James E. Black Pontiac-Cadillac in Cambria County. His loan was for more than $8,000. O'Kicki later, in a correspondence containing his official judicial letterhead, informed the bank that "there was no loan, there is no loan, there never shall be a loan." He indicated that he wouldn't help the bank with a trust dispute that had come before him in the county's orphans court unless the sales agreement and other documents were altered. O'Kicki ominously informed them that "my name is 'Judge.'" All documents related to this transaction were prepared for "Judge O'Kicki" with an address of "Courthouse, Ebensburg, PA."

The judge also pursued several questionable business ventures in spite of strict rules and regulations governing these activities for members of the judiciary. For instance, O'Kicki co-owned Richland Beer Distributor in Stonycreek Township with a man named Clarence Seftic. He used his wife's name to conceal his financial stake in the company, which was forbidden under Pennsylvania law.

In another instance, O'Kicki appeared to create a shell company for the sole purpose of giving the woman who became his second wife a break on car insurance.

At approximately 1:20 a.m. on February 19, 1982, the former Sylvia Duke and a passenger drove out of a motel parking lot along Route 119 in Indiana, traveling south in the northbound lane. Her vehicle collided head-on with another. She was charged with driving under the influence for the incident. Later that year, in October, she crashed yet again and faced the cancelation of her auto insurance policy because of her poor driving record.

The judge, however, started a business entity called Cambria Cemetery Services Inc. and listed the woman, his girlfriend, as a driver for the "company" car. Though Trigona was listed as president of the company, he testified that he was unaware that his name and signatures were on any of its paperwork. Bank witnesses said O'Kicki was the only person they dealt with in obtaining the loan for this car.

According to the grand jury presentment, the woman's risk factors meant that her insurance premium would have been approximately $1,850 per year. It was just $370 because of O'Kicki's involvement. The report noted that the judge had also submitted an affidavit vouching for her character in court, adding that this action may have violated Rule 1701(d) of the Pennsylvania

Supreme Court's Rules of Judicial Administration, which prohibits judges from voluntarily testifying as character witnesses.

The future Mrs. O'Kicki was ultimately enrolled in Accelerated Rehabilitative Disposition, better known as ARD, despite seeming to be ineligible for this program. ARD doles punishment to a defendant without an actual conviction. The program is designed for first offenders and can be attractive to defendants because it allows for the dismissal and expungement of charges.

A few years later, in 1986, O'Kicki contacted Ebensburg businessman Edwin Long to ask whether he had any rental property for sale. The two of them discussed Ebensburg Apartments. Long told the judge he would sell it for $400,000, but O'Kicki said the purchase price would have to be $440,000. O'Kicki then convinced James McConnell, an accounting professor whom he taught with at St. Francis University, and Dr. Sheonath Srivastava to offer a total of $440,000 to become co-owners of the apartments with O'Kicki. Long testified that he had a kickback agreement with the judge for facilitating the sale. O'Kicki received several thousands of dollars as a result of his secret arrangement with Long and stood to earn as much as $30,000 total.

Police believed O'Kicki was illegally mixing business with judicial matters in additional manners.

Frank J. Castelli appeared before O'Kicki in a case where the Pennsylvania Department of Transportation was constructing a roadway that impacted his property. His attorney argued that the doctrine of "assembled economic unit" would apply in this case. O'Kicki agreed, which increased Castelli's appraised loss from $440,000 to nearly $1 million.

Later, in July 1981, Castelli acted as guarantor for an O'Kicki loan from Laurel Bank. Financial records reflected that Castelli made interest payments on O'Kicki's loan and eventually paid a total of $7,500 toward the principal before the loan was paid off on January 7, 1987. Castelli said he agreed to this as part of an oral agreement with the judge to purchase a newspaper company owned by the judge.

The newspaper company, known as Mid-State News Inc., became defunct on March 30, 1981—four months before Castelli signed as guarantor on O'Kicki's loan. Castelli never received the company stock he was promised by the judge.

O'Kicki used $10,000 from the Laurel Bank loan toward a $27,000 investment to purchase and maintain the former Franklin school building in Franklin Borough, convincing prominent area businessman George Zamias and his wife, Marianna, to act as the straw party to conceal his involvement. Members of the Conemaugh Valley School Board ultimately agreed to sell the property for $15,000 instead of the original $25,000 asking price to Zamias Real Estate.

A solicitor for the school admitted that he had heard "rumors" that O'Kicki was involved with the purchase. "I can't say [they] would have had an impact on the court, but I knew I thought about it," the attorney testified.

According to O'Kicki's old friend Trigona, the judge had discussed converting the Franklin school to a white-collar crime detention center. O'Kicki had said he could use his position of influence within the judiciary to make this happen. He then convinced Craig Rolish, a friend of more than twenty years, to buy the property from Zamias for $50,000 without telling Rolish he was already owner of the facility.

Curiously, the judge also asked the Zamiases to give a portion of their proceeds from the agreement with Rolish to Johnstown women referred to as the "Oliverios" sisters. Trigona said the judge had borrowed $10,000 from the sisters in July 1981 after telling them he needed the money for tuition payments. O'Kicki, he added, had bragged about how he had "scammed" the sisters.

O'Kicki's relationship with the Zamias family was subject to other strange allegations in the report. The presentment noted that the judge had asked this family for a $40,000 loan to help him pay for his divorce in 1986. He later invited them to accompany him and his second wife, Sylvia Onusic, on their honeymoon. The Zamiases declined.

O'Kicki, however, wanted them to pay for the entire cost of the trip for the party of four: a ten-day romp in Europe. The listed price tag was $30,000. Instead, the Zamiases gave the newlyweds a $6,000 gift of cash. They also testified that they had provided the judge with expense-paid fishing trips to Michigan, Atlantic City, New Jersey and Mexico.

George Zamias additionally said that he noticed how O'Kicki always drove a "clunker" automobile and offered to help him buy a new one. The judge originally rebuffed the idea but later accepted somewhere between $6,000 and $9,000 from Zamias for a new car. Zamias said he continued to see the judge drive his old car in spite of the cash assistance.

O'Kicki, according to the grand jury report, used a vehicle owned by Cambria County auto dealer Ivan Wingard. The businessman told the state that he had discussed his son's criminal conviction and upcoming sentencing with the judge. Wingard admitted that he hoped loaning the car to O'Kicki would result in a lighter sentence for his son. The judge, after catching state police taking photographs of him exiting the vehicle at the courthouse on August 11, 1988, wrote to Wingard to inform him he was interested in formally purchasing the automobile.

Trigona also told investigators that O'Kicki once instructed him to solicit royalties from a man named Rudy Zucco after the judge approved a strip-mining operation on his property. He wanted somewhere between fifteen and twenty-five cents per ton that was mined. Zucco supposedly wanted no part of this and sold his interest to an entity called Interstate Fuels Inc.

The company that took over the planned operation was owned by area businessmen Frank Romani, Charles Brazil and Anthony Capretti. Two investors testified that they gave $3,000 each to Romani, who said he used it to "take care of Judge." Later, in the summer of 1983, Trigona asked O'Kicki about the bribe money. The judge told him he didn't have it all yet but showed him a pair of $5,000 IOU notes signed by Romani.

The grand jury report noted that O'Kicki maintained as many as fifty-four bank accounts from the years 1979 through 1988.

Allegations of wrongdoing surrounded O'Kicki's campaign for Pennsylvania Superior Court as well. Interstate Fuels partners Brazil and Capretti testified that they act gave O'Kicki $100 cash as a contribution to his statewide campaign for the Pennsylvania Superior Court. These donations did not appear in the judge's campaign expense reports

According to Trigona, the judge had said "one of the reasons that he was running [for Superior Court] was that he could use some of the campaign money to keep afloat." Trigona told investigators he used cash campaign contributions during this time to pay bills for the judge at O'Kicki's behest.

Also referenced was a "testimonial" dinner for the judge that took place in June 1987. This was held at the Northfork Country Club and was intended, according to the indictment, to help the judge pay off his outstanding debts. Area insurance broker Joseph Voltz helped organize the event, which was attended by three attorneys, the owner of a court reporting service, the managing partner of a firm of certified public accountants and other prominent locals. The charge was $500 per plate, and it generated approximately $6,000 for the judge.

A year later, just a few days before he was sworn in as president judge, O'Kicki made a ruling in orphans court that cut attorney fees chargeable against an estate in half. This helped Voltz directly, as he was a one-quarter beneficiary. The ruling meant Voltz would receive an extra $9,625.

According to the presentment:

The Grand Jury found it to be of considerable significance that Joseph Voltz, who had initiated and facilitated the collection of some $6,000.00 in order to help Judge O'Kicki pay his debts, would have received a benefit of thousands of dollars, his share of the Sharkey estate, as a result of Judge O'Kicki's May 27, 1988 ruling, had O'Kicki not subsequently vacated his order of that date.

The report stated that on May 28, a day after the Voltz ruling, the judge became somehow aware of the state police inquiry. O'Kicki then handed Voltz a check for $5,000 on June 3, 1988, to distribute to those who had helped pay his bills through the testimonial dinner fundraiser. This was the same day as his inauguration as president judge of Cambria County. On June 6, just a few days later, O'Kicki met with a state police officer he knew to ask what the trooper could discover about the grand jury investigation. The judge wanted to know which individual officers were assigned to the case. He also asked the officer if he would contact the deputy attorney general assigned to the probe and, after asking for details about the case, report back to him. The trooper declined the judge's request and instead told his supervisors and the investigators about his conversation with O'Kicki.

That same day, O'Kicki attempted to undo and vacate the May 27 order that had benefited Voltz.

Another aspect of the report stemming from the 1987 fundraiser was an alleged bid-rigging. A member of O'Kicki's staff asked Sara Sargent if she would like to bid on providing court reporting services for a series of asbestos cases soon to be heard in the Cambria County Court of Common Pleas. Sargent's group at that time didn't do much court reporting work in Cambria County. She then spoke with the judge approximately ten months after the fundraiser. O'Kicki apparently advised her to lower her bid rate of $145 per day to $75 per day. He instructed her "to adjust [her bidder rate] but not adjust it too drastically because [she] was going to get the business anyway." Sargent later received the contract, and from the spring of 1988 through September 30 of that year, her company billed both the county and private counsel handling O'Kicki's assigned asbestos cases a total of $9,656.88.

The grand jury made note that an attorney who attended the judge's fundraiser was appointed as the orphans court master, despite having never practiced in this discipline of the law.

In its concluding pages, the presentment recounted a strange episode involving one of O'Kicki's rental properties. The report stated that an illegal water line tap led from a residence owned by a man named Charles Kist. It led into an adjacent mobile home that the judge rented out.

Rudy Bozic, the man who dug the water line to the judge's trailer, testified that O'Kicki paid for the material for the illegal extension and that a backhoe was loaned to the judge by a local heavy equipment company. O'Kicki supposedly did not pay for his labor. Asked why he did the work for free, Bozic said he expected the judge to help him if he ever had legal problems. Then he wrote in 1983 that he was unaware of the illegal tap entirely.

In 1985, the connection was removed by the water authority, but it was reinstalled later. O'Kicki allegedly called water authority enforcement officer Ralph Horner in the fall of that year to threaten him with jail if he didn't stop intervening in the water line matter.

Properly extending the line, according to the grand jury, would have cost the judge approximately $5,000.

<hr />

Through the lens of the presentment, O'Kicki was a man unworthy of the bench and deserving of prison. He was at best a liar, cheat and backstabber and at worst a dangerous and tyrannical power monger willing to subvert justice if it would enhance his personal holdings.

Absent from the voluminous charges, however, was even an abstract reference to gambling—which was, according to Trooper Walt Komoroski, the entire pretext for the state police investigation. To some, this omission raised a significant question about the case: Why were authorities suddenly concerned about gambling rumors in Cambria County after decades of looking the other way?

Chapter 5

JOHNSTOWN VICE

I n the late 1970s, Westmont native Neil Price was attending a University of Pittsburgh at Johnstown forum on the assassination of John F. Kennedy. It was here that he first met Judge Joseph O'Kicki. Price went on to practice law in Cambria County, and he, like many others, took notice when O'Kicki was suspended amid the sensational allegations. Later, he would assist the judge with his legal defense because he believed the commonwealth's case was thin in some regards. To this day, he believes investigators' illegal gambling suspicions were a false pretext.

"It's peculiar that the police would rely on that as being their lynchpin to start a grand jury," the long-haired, soft-spoken attorney said.

According to Price, O'Kicki may have been suspected in part because of prior rulings. He had dismissed illegal gambling charges against several individuals earlier that decade.

"O'Kicki said, 'Bring your evidence to court and we'll work with what you got. But if you don't have enough, you shouldn't be getting warrants,'" Price said.

"The judges shouldn't be rubber stamps for this sort of thing…especially if they consider gambling problem so bad in this part of 'Pennsyltucky' that they would decide [it's] worthy of a grand jury."

Vice was indeed a longtime fixture of Johnstown. The city, like many others in America, had a deeply ingrained gambling culture that took hold around the turn of the twentieth century when immigrants from central and eastern Europe flocked to the region for steel and coal jobs.

Dice, sports betting, high-stakes card games and underground lotteries could be found in establishments across Johnstown, Altoona and other western Pennsylvania cities. Elements of the Mafia provided the backbone and structure for much of it.

Leland Wood's education about the mob began in earnest when he was hired as a reporter for the *Johnstown Tribune-Democrat* newspaper in August 1975. Working night hours at the Locust Street office, he remembered the first time a gravelly voiced man asked him for the balance of the U.S. Treasury.

Neil Price, who helped Judge O'Kicki with some of his legal work, sitting down for a 2019 interview at the *Daily American* newspaper office in Somerset. *Photo by Eric Kieta/*Daily American.

Wood said he was puzzled by the question. The newspaper printed the balance, a long string of numbers, each day for reasons he didn't understand—until some coworkers explained. "They'd just snicker. 'That was the mob.' I was told they were taking the last digits of the treasury balance and that was the [winning] numbers," Wood said.

"It was an easy quick way of picking the number."

Wood's tenure at the paper continued into the 1980s. He recalled vociferously reading the annual Pennsylvania Crime Commission reports for story leads about the Mafia and its influence on the region. His understanding of the mob's games and money laundering helped him produce article after article, particularly after he took over as the paper's Blair County beat.

"That was a competitive nightmare for my competitors," he said with a chuckle.

One of those stories emerged when Wood discovered a public notice in the *Altoona Mirror* newspaper for Jaye's Bar. He knew the significance of the bar because of the Pennsylvania Crime Commission's annual reports. The April 1981 edition connected Jaye's with known mobster John Verilla, a man who would later be convicted of orchestrating the 1979 murder of drug dealer and Mafia associate John H. Clark. Verilla had ordered two men to shoot Clark, deemed a liability to the crime family, somewhere in Cambria County. "Let them have the garbage," Verilla reportedly said.

The report stated:

> *His wife, Angeline C. Verilla, is the co-owner of Jaye's Bar, 1208 16th Street, Altoona. Jaye's has been cited for gambling activity by the*

Shown here at left is Johnstown City Hall. Two buildings down is the former City Cigar shop, once a headquarters for local Mafia activity. *Photo by Bruce Siwy.*

Pennsylvania Liquor Control Board and the owners' application for a transfer of the liquor license to 201–15 East Sixth Avenue, Altoona, has been withheld pending the outcome of the citation....The incidence of crime in Pennsylvania is expected to remain at unacceptably high levels and could even increase in the next year. Organized crime, in particular, shows no sign of abatement in the Commonwealth.

Wood said Jaye's employees were to attend a Pennsylvania Liquor Control Board hearing for engaging in behavior prohibited to license holders—namely, illegal gambling.

"They put the two state troopers, undercover guys, on the witness stand. They were in the bar at different times," Wood said. "What they described was the bartender frequently answering the phone and writing numbers down on a notepad or scrap paper. [They] concluded that the behavior was a numbers operation."

Wood said the bartender denied being part of a numbers racket. He told the administrative judge he simply passed information along to an elderly woman who was a shut-in and didn't have access to it. The bartender's story

A closer look at City Cigar along Main Street in Johnstown. *Photo by Bruce Siwy.*

was not aggressively questioned or scrutinized, leaving Wood to believe that the enforcement attorney was either inept or unwilling to cross a mob-connected outfit.

"The fact that some people do things that are clearly illegal and they do it for money is no revelation to anybody who's grown up," Wood said.

According to that 1981 Pennsylvania Crime Commission report, the commonwealth spent $1.5 million to combat Mafia and mob-like activity in 1980 alone. The majority, 71 percent, was used for the salaries and benefits of investigators. Authors of the report noted that mob activity remained robust at this time, especially on the east side of Pennsylvania.

"Not since the years surrounding Prohibition has a gangland war happened in Philadelphia of the magnitude of the one which has been occurring," they wrote. "The incidence of crime in Pennsylvania is expected to remain at unacceptably high levels and could even increase in the next year. Organized crime, in particular, shows no sign of abatement in the Commonwealth."

According to the commission, the indisputable crime boss on the western side of Pennsylvania was John Sebastian LaRocca. His rap sheet included theft, gambling and violence, beginning with a 1922 arrest for assault with intent to kill and maim, earning him a three- to five-year prison sentence. He was fined $300 and given a year's probation for operating an illegal lottery in 1939 and fined $100 a year later for stealing automobile license plates.

In 1956, the U.S. Immigration and Naturalization Service began deportation proceedings for the gritty mobster, dubbing the Italian an "undesirable alien." Pennsylvania governor John S. Fine, however, curiously granted LaRocca a backdated pardon. The deportation case was dropped.

It was around this time, the commission stated, that LaRocca succeeded Frank Amato Sr. of Braddock and formally took the reins of an organized crime empire that stretched from Altoona to the West Virginia panhandle. He was identified as part of a Mafia clique that included Frank Rosa, Joseph Sica and Gabriel "Kelly" Mannerino.

In 1962, LaRocca was arrested and fined fifty dollars for carrying a concealed weapon. He and several others were indicted by a federal grand jury in New York before the end of the decade for refereeing a dispute over which crime family would receive kickbacks from a Teamsters pension fund. He was ultimately acquitted.

LaRocca's influence was prevalent in the region's business world. He owned a car wash on Pittsburgh's Northside and maintained homes in both McCandless and Pompano Beach, Florida. Unsealed FBI records sourced by the *Tribune-Review* in 1996 implied that Art Rooney Sr.—beloved owner of the Pittsburgh Steelers professional football franchise—handed off a slot machine empire to LaRocca sometime in the 1940s or '50s. An informant told the FBI that Rooney "controlled the entire Pittsburgh vicinity in this regard" before LaRocca became king.

Johnstown and its suburbs of the mid-twentieth century—awash with money from the steel boom—were among the jewels LaRocca counted within his network until his death in 1984.

IN 1971, NAMES AND details of Mafia operations in the city of Johnstown became public as the result of a Pennsylvania Crime Commission hearing. Johnstown mobster Clarence "Mutt" Lewis testified under immunity that recently deceased Frank Mikesic had controlled the syndicate's "franchises" of local gambling operators, ran the local mob's "taxation" of gambling activities and distributed the funds in the form of "contributions" to gain political influence in the city. He characterized Mikesic as the "big man in crooked politics."

"Mikesic was very much in politics, not on one side or the other," Lewis said in an article reported by the *Pittsburgh Press*. "Mikesic was in politics right up to the hilt and he supported candidates that were 'non-reformists.' Let's put it that way."

The article noted that a few months after Mikesic's death, his widow's home was burglarized. A wall safe was found to have been removed from a closet in his former bedroom. Members of the crime commission theorized that the break-in was conducted to prevent investigators from discovering incriminating evidence on others who were involved in Mikesic's activities.

"Furs, television sets and other expensive objects were left untouched," the commission wrote. "Mrs. Mikesic advised the local authorities that the safe contained two passbooks for local bank accounts and some of her husband's papers, the contents of which she was not aware."

As a result of the commission's findings—which included 1,500 pages of sworn testimony from thirty-four witnesses—Johnstown police chief Sam Coco was handed a ten-day suspension for "incompetence, malfeasance and misfeasance" in office. He resigned and was replaced by Captain Fred Lydic.

"Managers of gambling enterprises who made contributions to Mikesic were notified in advance of impending local raids," the commission alleged. "Gamblers who refused to contribute were raided without prior notice."

Additionally, the commission concluded that former Johnstown mayor Kenneth O. Tompkins had "reflected a lack of concern for the existence of organized gambling and an unsatisfactory record of combatting it." Tompkins had been convicted after pleading guilty to accepting a bribe from Tele-Prompter Corp. as part of a conspiracy for the company to obtain the cable TV franchise in the area. The Associated Press noted that Tompkins was called to testify under oath.

But if Tompkins had anything to offer the commission, he was in no mood to share it: "I have been asked here as a guest and I have no comment to make."

Other "guests" and witnesses at the hearing included former nightclub owner Richard L. Williams, bartender Peter Duranko, Kline's Amusements owner Edward Kline, nightclub employee Russell F. Wallace, Nicholas Sikirica, "unemployed Johnstown man" Samuel Verrone and Samuel Fasciano, co-operator of the Shangri-La Lounge and Restaurant, located just outside the city. Fasciano told a reporter, "Ask [the crime commission].... They have all the answers" when asked about his presence there.

Four other notables were subpoenaed: LaRocca; Johnstown mob lieutenant "Little" Joe Regino; John L. LaRocca, brother to LaRocca and partner with Regino in a Johnstown amusement company; and Johnstown bond salesman George Bondy.

LaRocca and Regino also reportedly owned a cigarette vending company called Keystone Sales. The commission alleged that underworld "summit" meetings were routinely held at the Shangri-La—a venue cited later by O'Kicki in writings to federal authorities.

Conflicts within and between these sorts of outfits were sometimes resolved with beatings and bloodshed. A 1984 article from the *Pittsburgh Press* headlined "Long Arm of Crime: Murder Trial in Cambria Shows Extent of Pittsburgh Underworld's Influence" provides an anecdote of this casual violence. Vincent Caracciolo told authorities that he and John Clark—a Salvation Army worker who moonlighted as a drug pusher—used a van to pick up a man named John McDermott on an Altoona street corner in 1978. McDermott had run afoul of the mob for setting up a competing numbers racket. So the "mobsters whacked off [his] pinky finger with a machete and eventually flicked it out a car window like a cigarette butt."

"Fear keeps everything going," Caracciolo testified. He said his boss, John "Jack" Verilla, was so excited by the finger-chopping news that he nearly called his superiors in Pittsburgh but decided against it because it was late at night. Caracciolo briefly considered keeping the finger as a trophy before tossing it.

For his part, McDermott said nothing. He told police he had been unconscious and never saw his attackers.

A year later, "LaRocca soldier" Caracciolo was at work again, this time on former colleague Clark. He said Clark was angry after being cut out of Verilla's drug operations. He threatened to "flip."

Caracciolo, on Verilla's orders, drove Clark to a remote area of Cambria County and buried an axe in his skull. Then he set both Clark and his vehicle on fire.

"I admired Jack, respected him, loved him. He treated me special and made me feel important," Caracciolo said, characterizing Verilla as the head of Altoona's Cosa Nostra fiefdom. "Whatever Jack Verilla wanted me to do, I'd do it for him. If it was dumb, I'd still do it.

"I'm afraid of Jack Verilla and the people behind him. You can't hide from him."

In his book *Smalltime: A Story of My Family and the Mob*, Cambria County native Russell Shorto details some of these organized crime activities with

the assistance of some older gentlemen who lived through the rise of these operations. Men like the LaRoccas and Regino were aided and abetted, Shorto's sources said, by a network of politicians, police, prosecutors and judges willing to look away for the right price. He quoted Caram Abood—a former Cambria County district attorney and the judge who sat at O'Kicki's right hand during his president judge inauguration—about a "very straightforward payoff system" that kept the system running smoothly.

A decades-old photo of Caram Abood. *Courtesy of the* Altoona Mirror.

Though Abood declined through a law partner to comment for this book, he told Shorto:

[The mob] *paid 5 percent of their take to whichever party was in power in the county, and in exchange they were left alone. Whenever an election was coming up, the party would call and say, "The DA is going to be sending some officers. You should have someone at each of your shops, and you should have a few dollars and a few numbers tickets around." Somebody had to take the fall. Then once they were at the county courthouse, they would be sure to get the guy in front of Judge Nelson. Judge Nelson was the friendly judge. "Well, nobody got hurt. How do you plead? Guilty? A hundred dollar fine." And that would be it.*

The idea that "somebody had to take the fall" is one that's been echoed by O'Kicki's supporters. Many who publicly supported him amid his legal troubles continue to stand by him decades later. Time, context and perspective have not altered their perception of the situation. They seem to believe firmly and truly that state police were tipped off and unleashed on O'Kicki by individuals with ulterior motives.

The judge himself, of course, fanned those sorts of flames from nearly the outset of his suspension. An example is his February 24, 1989 appeal for help from the Pennsylvania Conference of State Trial Judges officers. He wrote in a memo using his official judicial letterhead:

FIRST, no person (President of the United States, judge, AOPC employee, attorney, policeman, legislator, or person) is above the law. The only exceptions to this rule in our society are newspaper reporters, editors, publishers and owners of the media.

SECOND, how many judges can withstand an intensive re-examination, re-editing of the facts, and reinterpretation of law as it applies to virtually every public, financial, business and personal act for the past 20 years?... How many of you would appreciate your mother-in-law being subpoenaed and then asked by the Attorney General before the Grand Jury when you first dated her daughter, ETC.? Every divorced judge in Pennsylvania is in peril! This peril comes from present as well as former mother-in-laws.

According to O'Kicki, exculpatory evidence was being ignored as police narrowed their inquiry to speaking with everyone who "hates [my] guts." He expressed outrage that grand jury testimony—confidential by law— was leaking into newspaper accounts, and he downplayed his use of official letterhead on personal correspondences and his habit of asking county secretaries to write memos for him. O'Kicki opined that that most other judges have done the same.

"The hell with O'Kicki. Let him fight his own battle," O'Kicki wrote. "Ask yourself this question: WHICH OF YOU IS NEXT?"

Thus began a theme for O'Kicki: he would go on to blame his problems on political powerbrokers with mob connections.

"I am a maverick. I don't owe any allegiance to any political party," he told the Associated Press in 1989.

"The various political factions just can't tolerate that, and they can't tolerate the reformer I was. Someone has pushed the state police button. I'm not sure who, but I'm working on it."

O'Kicki later detailed these allegations in letters, memos and the outline for a tell-all memoir. First, however, he would focus on fighting for his freedom and for his life.

Chapter 6

LEVY AND GRIFO

The *Commonwealth v. Joseph O'Kicki* quickly attained international infamy, touching off a media circus that included reports from the *New York Times*, the *Los Angeles Times* and Bill O'Reilly of *Inside Edition*. The soundtrack for this circus might well have been a parody jingle that hit local airwaves. It was set to the music and melody of Toni Basil's "Hey Mickey" and included the following verse:

O'Kicki, what a pity / You might be a swine
They say you broke the law / So you might be doin' time

When the charges were filed in the spring of 1989, the suspended president judge of Cambria County immediately posted the money to satisfy the $10,000 bail and began to devise his defense. He first consulted with an old acquaintance: Cambria County's current president judge, Norman A. Krumenacker III, who was practicing law as an attorney at that time.

"The thing that everybody ran into in representing Joe [O'Kicki] was… he had his conspiratorial theory about this whole thing. You know, he was the victim of a conspiracy," Krumenacker said. "The only problem was the evidence was rather overwhelming.

"And, in respect to my profession, I cannot tell you what our legal advice was to him at the time, even though he's passed, but it was clear that our advice of how to proceed was inconsistent with his desires."

Unhappy with Krumenacker's counsel, O'Kicki instead hired attorneys L. Edward Glass and David Weaver.

As the proceedings were set, observers from all over began offering their insights. Reporter Carol Morello's article in the April 30, 1989 edition of the *Edmonton Journal* noted that "while O'Kicki is listed as the sole defendant, the grand jury presentment is viewed here as a broader indictment of some of Cambria County's most upright and trusted citizens and institutions.… For more than a decade, if the allegations are true, numerous lawyers, court employees, bankers, businessmen and other pillars of the community kept their mouths shut while they watched a man who had pledged to uphold the law trample over it. For more than a decade in which O'Kicki is alleged to have been a liar, a cheat, a thief and a bully, virtually no one complained."

The story included comments from Cambria County commissioner Ron Stephenson. "Obviously, the presentment indicates one member of the judiciary gone amok," Stephenson said in the article. "But it also does not speak well of the bar association and the banking community. The average man on the street is appalled by the revelations."

Delaware County senior judge Melvin Levy was chosen to preside over the case. He, like O'Kicki's defenders, did not appear to be impressed by some of the prosecution's claims. Levy dismissed two charges against the judge in May 1989. These were related to whether O'Kicki had attempted to influence the 1982 drunken driving case against his former girlfriend and current wife.

The commonwealth failed to presence evidence that O'Kicki had taken any substantial step toward obstructing the administration of justice, Levy said. He declined to comment on whether O'Kicki had violated any code of ethics, noting that this question was "for another forum to decide."

Lawrence Claus, who was prosecuting the case on behalf of Pennsylvania attorney general Ernest Preate, indicated that he was not discouraged by the dismissals. "Anytime you go into a preliminary hearing, you run the risk of a ruling that the evidence does not justify a charge," he said in an Associated Press report. "Obviously, the commonwealth felt it had a case."

Soon, however, prosecutors would walk away from dozens of other charges against the judge. The *Pittsburgh Press* reported that forty of the seventy-six counts against O'Kicki were withdrawn just two months after his indictment. A few others were dismissed outright.

The allegation that the judge had used his position to coerce First United Federal to forgive thousands of dollars in loans to District Judge Max

Pavlovich was among those that wilted under scrutiny. Levy said "there was no scintilla of evidence" against O'Kicki for that count.

Charges retained against O'Kicki included various counts for calling two secretaries into his office while he wore only undershorts; forcing two former tipstaffs to do chores for the judge on county time and on weekends; soliciting bribes from attorney Richard J. Green in a zoning case; owning a beer distributorship in violation of the Liquor Control Act; forging the name of former tipstaff Tony Trigona on documents; soliciting a kickback on the purchase of a property in Ebensburg; circumventing the law in obtaining municipal water for a trailer he owned; and offering to act on an estate matter for Laurel Bank if the bank took care of his "personal matters" by reducing one of his loans.

For Claus, this would be one of several high-profile cases he'd prosecute during his lengthy career. His credentials would later include the conviction of former state Supreme Court justice Joan Orie Melvin in 2013. Orie Melvin was found guilty of theft of services for forcing state-funded employees to work on her election campaigns in both 2003 and 2009.

Looking back on the O'Kicki case, Claus said not to read too far into the early avalanche of dropped and dismissed charges against the judge.

> *That's not an unusual situation. In fact…it sticks in my mind* [that] *there may have been as many as seventy-six counts that were handed down by the grand jury. And when you go to the first stage of a criminal prosecution, which is the preliminary hearing, a district magistrate judge, or in this case a judge from the Court of Common Pleas—who was specially appointed by the Pennsylvania Supreme Court—has a responsibility to determine if there's enough proof for a case or cases to go forward. So it's not actually that unusual to find some cases or some counts being dismissed. I think the best way to look at it is sometimes the issuing authority handling the preliminary hearing look towards streamlining a case, moving things to where the more serious charges can proceed unhampered.*
>
> *We did lose…I believe there were six counts that were thrown out at the preliminary hearing, and I do remember there's probably another group of charges that we withdrew so that we would have a much more streamlined case to go to trial.*

The momentum for the defense, however, was palpable to those in O'Kicki's corner. His widow, Sylvia Onusic, said she felt some optimism in the early proceedings.

Judge Abood was appointed acting president judge [of Cambria County]. And he put in a request for an outside judge [to come] and hear the preliminary objections and take care of the preliminary parts of the trial. We didn't know Judge Levy at all, but when he came on the bench he had a presence. He was really a professional jurist. And during the preliminary hearing he had several law clerks working for him and he would tell the law clerk, "Get me this, get me that." They would go in the law library and bring books. He had law books piled up on his desk. He was checking different cases and the outcomes. And he was very professional.

I said [to my husband], "No matter what happens, I'm very happy with Judge Levy. He seems to be a true jurist and not a political tool of somebody."

But Levy's time with this case would be short. By July, he had recused himself after being urged—some say threatened—to step away.

THE FIRST MOTION FOR recusal filed by Claus was benign. He and his office expressed concern that Levy wouldn't have enough time to give these hearings the attention they deserved. They suggested that Levy's court schedule was too crowded.

When this motion was ignored, Claus and the attorney general's office increased the pressure. They filed a supplementary motion for recusal on July 3, 1989. Cited was a "concern that the hardship encountered by the instant Court—who must travel hundreds of miles to the situs of the anticipated trial—could bring about a lack of objectivity by this Honorable Court when it comes to a full consideration and fair hearing of the remaining issues at hand at the pre-trial, trial, and post-trial stages of the above-captioned case."

Additionally, the prosecution accused Levy of "an apparent pre-disposition" against some of O'Kicki's charges. The supplemental motion for recusal noted that Levy injected questions sixty-three times during the preliminary hearing, and it cited statements Levy made to two Cambria County sheriff's deputies, Ray Bargas and Linda Speicher, as evidence of bias. Levy allegedly told Bargas and Speicher that he had some "tricks up his sleeve" to shorten the proceedings.

In an affidavit signed June 26, 1989, Bargas wrote: "As we were proceeding from the airport toward Pittsburgh, in casual conversation I asked Judge Levy how long he thought he might be staying? He replied that he should not be staying too long. He stated he had some tricks up his sleeve. And, it was not necessary to convict a person on all charges to establish a conviction."

Levy also apparently commented to Senior Deputy Attorney General Paul E. von Geis Jr. that the prosecution didn't "need all of those charges.... All you [the Commonwealth] need is one to get him off the bench and that's all that is important."

Claus and the prosecution also went beyond questioning Levy's predisposition to the case. They noted that O'Kicki was being charged in part for using his judicial letterhead on correspondences for his own personal matters—and that they found evidence that Levy, too, was guilty of the same.

Their motion stated:

> *Certain documents have come to the attention of the Attorney General's Office (as the same are evidenced by photocopies of two separate letters bearing the name of Your Honorable Court, each dated June 5, 1987, and both of which are attached hereto as Exhibits D and E) that appear to reveal the use of correspondence upon the official letterhead of your Honorable Court and which are of special concern.... The Commonwealth submits that the existence of these documents substantiates a perception held by the Commonwealth that this Honorable Court might not rule with impartiality and objectivity upon those respective remaining matters to be litigated concerning this case.*

In their evidentiary exhibits, the prosecutors had copies of letters that Levy had sent to a commissioner and an attorney with the Pennsylvania Bureau of Professional and Occupational Affairs in 1987. The judge appeared to demand resolution of a personal complaint lodged against a medical professional dating back to 1982. These messages indeed were written using Levy's official judicial letterhead.

So on July 25, 1989, a few weeks after the second recusal request, Levy announced that he was stepping away. He cited having a substantial number of previously scheduled criminal and civil trials back home—and the likelihood of one or more trials being necessary in the O'Kicki case—as his reason for leaving.

If mentioning Levy's use of judicial letterhead in personal correspondence was intended by prosecution as a veiled threat, the tactic was successful. Levy abruptly had no time for O'Kicki.

LEVY'S RECUSAL WAS ONE of several controversies that arose in this case. The defense team cried foul, noting that the motions were presented privately outside the public record. They accused the prosecution of glaring misconduct. O'Kicki attorneys L. Edward Glass and David Weaver said the attorney general's office had improperly coerced Levy off the case, causing a "chilling effect" on judges presiding over this and other criminal trials. Their cries were eventually heard by the national media and a wide-ranging audience.

Bill O'Reilly, the conservative author and political commentator of Fox News fame, once played host to the alternative news show *Inside Edition*. He and reporter Rick Kirkham produced a segment on the O'Kicki scandal in the early 1990s. The report focused on the prosecution's strong suggestion for Levy to walk away from the case.

Pennsylvania attorney general Ernest Preate was interviewed as part of the story. He bristled at the notion that his office had pressured Levy in this matter in an exchange with Kirkham.

> *Preate: "No, the judge recused himself from the case. There was a pretrial conference scheduled by the judge, after the preliminary hearing [and] before the trial. That's normal."*
>
> *Kirkham: "But the judge would have stepped down prior to his preliminary hearing decisions had he felt that he was not the appropriate judge to preside over this. In fact, state agents presented him with the idea that he should step down. Is that not correct?"*
>
> *Preate: "Well, that was made based on some comments the judge had made during the preliminary hearing—"*
>
> *Kirkham: "But the state did suggest that the judge step down?"*
>
> *Preate: "We suggested it to him. That's our obligation."*

Having reviewed the pretrial motions from the attorney general's office decades after they were filed, Ebensburg defense attorney Tim Burns said he was a little bothered by the prosecution's behavior.

> *In regards to Judge Levy, I really don't feel he committed any acts or anything that would have warranted a recusal. In the legal profession, judges are like people. You've got some judges that are very straight-laced [and] some are a little outgoing—gregarious may be the word. And that's*

Tim Burns, a Johnstown attorney with a law office in Ebensburg, discusses the O'Kicki case at the Venue of Merging Arts, aka VOMA, in Cambria City. *Photo by Eric Kieta/*Daily American.

what I picture Judge Levy being, as the type of judge that maybe jokes or maybe is a little outgoing.

The attorney general was upset that he made a comment in chambers—that means in the judge's office—that all you need is one conviction to get Judge O'Kicki removed from the bench. I don't feel that was out of line or showing a bias: it was a fact. That's all you needed was one conviction. They filed dozens of charges against him. I think the attorney general at the time [and] the prosecuting attorneys were probably just very sensitive to the seriousness of the matter. They wanted to get a conviction.

In hindsight, Claus maintains that he and the attorney general's office took the appropriate action.

To be quite honest with you, I think that [Levy] was out of Delaware County, and I remember going down to Delaware County with the state police and bringing this subject up to Judge Levy—of course in the presence of [his] defense counsel—and pointed out that we had heard from not just state police, but other law enforcement, comments made and made by the judge that made it appear as if he had pre-judged certain parts of the case. And what we were asking was either he consider recusing himself or, you know, if necessary we would ask for a hearing.

Well, he recused himself.

Levy was replaced by Senior Judge Richard Grifo, a jurist from Northampton County. Grifo was promptly asked to consider a pretrial motion from O'Kicki's team arguing that the prosecution had lacked jurisdiction to empanel the investigating grand jury. Their contention was that statewide grand juries could be used only when there was evidence of a multi-county crime conspiracy.

Claus, then and now, dismissed this argument as a faulty one.

> Under the new state grand jury act—and when I say "new," that would have been taken effect in the early 1980s—grand juries had that argument made against them by defense counsel representing people who were presented upon. We don't use the word "indictment" [because] at that time the investigating grand jury [handed] down a "presentment." But at that time it was one of the arguments that the defense counsel would make. And early on the courts said, "No, under the grand jury act and under the rules of criminal procedure for grand juries...it's not limited to organized crime."
>
> A county, for example, that just didn't have the financial wherewithal to put into effect a grand jury could bring their cases to the attorney general. And that happened quite frequently, I know personally, during my fifteen years of tenure there.

To counter the defense's pretrial motion, Claus filed a brief in September 1989 that would grab front-page headlines. From the *Altoona Mirror*:

> State police disclosed to the attorney general's office that defendant O'Kicki, while a judge, visited an establishment where acts of prostitution allegedly occurred and it was reported that the said judge participated in activities with the women who worked there. Further, it was alleged that the same location had been identified as a place in which illegal drugs, including cocaine and marijuana, were sold.

These claims added another salacious twist to the case and would be aggressively challenged by O'Kicki's attorney. The defense would taunt the prosecution to bring forward the evidence of these brothel visits—evidence that never surfaced.

Later, O'Kicki and Price obtained a sworn and notarized affidavit from lifelong Old Conemaugh Boro resident Charles Barrett, former watchman and groundskeeper of a place called Rachel's. This establishment at 765–67 Cottage Place was well known to locals as a house of prostitution just outside the Johnstown city limits. Barrett confirmed that he was familiar with who O'Kicki was but never saw him at the establishment.

AFFIDAVIT OF CHARLES A. BARRETT

COMMONWEALTH OF PENNSYLVANIA:
                              :SS:
COUNTY   OF   CAMBRIA:

                        I, CHARLES A. BARRETT, of
150 Singer Street, Johnstown PA and a lifelong resident
of the Old Conemaugh Borough neighborhood, being duly
sworn, herein depose and say:

                        For nearly twenty years, I
have been a close and trusted friend of RACHEL YOUNG
and MILTON YOUNG, the former owners of "Rachel's", on
765-767 Cottage Place. They are now deceased. I was both
their groundskeeper, as well as one of the gentlemen
serving as a watchman for their establishment.

                        I have known Judge Joseph O'
Kicki since when he was an attorney. Judge O'Kicki never
visited the Rachel establishment on Cottage Place or anywhere else. The stories about Judge O'Kicki visiting the
brothels are fabrications. The stories about Judge O"Kicki
protecting the Rachel establishment are also plain lies.
I would know whether or not either story was true or
not, due to my position of trust with the Young family
and their business, and the stories of an O'Kicki connection are simply plain lies.

                        The above information is true
and correct to the best of my knowledge, information and
belief. I am aware of both the civil and criminal penalties for furnishing false information or making false
statements of this type.

DATE: March 22, 1990

                              _____
                              CHARLES A. BARRETT

SWORN AND SUBSCRIBED
BEFORE ME ON THIS 22
OF MARCH, 1990

_____
NOTARY PUBLIC

In a notarized 1990 affidavit, the groundskeeper for Rachel's infamous house of prostitution asserted that Judge Joseph O'Kicki never visited the establishment. *Courtesy of Sylvia Onusic.*

"I have known Judge Joseph O'Kicki since when he was an attorney. Judge O'Kicki never visited the Rachel establishment on Cottage Place or anywhere else," Barrett wrote in an affidavit signed March 22, 1990.

"The stories about Judge O'Kicki visiting the brothels are fabrications. The stories about Judge O'Kicki protecting the Rachel establishment are plain lies. I would know whether or not either story was true or not, due to my position of trust with the Young family and their business, and the stories of an O'Kicki connection are simply plain lies."

Onusic pointed out that O'Kicki was never charged with any vice-type crimes. She said:

In order to secure a grand jury, the cops—the police—have to write a statement of probable cause. And in this statement of probable cause, which we got much later, they indicated gambling, prostitution, racketeering, insurance fraud…yet there was not one charge in O'Kicki's presentment or in any of the proceedings on any of these charges. So our attorneys disputed this improper empanelment of the grand jury to investigate O'Kicki, but they said, "Oh, we came across it just by chance."

Meanwhile, it was very deliberate. People were getting subpoenas and so on very early on.

Nonetheless, Grifo sided with the prosecution. He dismissed the lack of jurisdiction objections, and the case proceeded to trial.

The jury pool for the case was drawn from the Cambria County area, another point of contention for O'Kicki and his team. O'Kicki claimed that one of the eventual jurors had a son who appeared before him in court, and another had a niece who had appeared before him in court. He questioned whether they could be impartial because of this. "Virtually all of the jurors… clearly established that the publicity is so pervasive so as to prevent a fair trial," an attorney for the judge said in seeking a mistrial.

His defense counsel would also later write that "because the trial court judge lived 200 miles away from the site of the alleged crimes he had no sense of feeling for the hostile climate that was created by the local news media.…During jury selection, the trial court remarked that he received the news clippings supplied by the Administrative Office of Pennsylvania Courts. Thus, having read the biased, prejudiced and false stories printed by the *Johnstown Tribune Democrat*, the judge already had a biased opinion against the Defendant."

Burns, again, said the defense may have had a point. "When you go to trial you want a jury pool that's reflective of your local community, plus is non-biased, is objective [and] has no knowledge of the proceedings—or, if they do, they won't hold that against the person," Burns said. "I feel it was a no-brainer that it should have been an out-of-county jury. Period."

In addition to the local radio station's "Hey Mickey" parody song that lampooned the judge, Burns recalled an O'Kicki lookalike contest being sponsored by the Johnstown Chiefs semi-pro hockey team.

"I mean, we can laugh about it, but it shows you how…'tainted' is the word, that your jury pool would be. So there should have been a jury from out of the county," he said.

Members of the non-sequestered jury—which included a copy editor from the *Tribune-Democrat*, a local newspaper that had printed the grand jury presentment verbatim and extensively covered the scandal—admitted having knowledge of the case. They told Grifo, however, that they could leave their personal opinions out of it and focus on whether the charges had merit.

O'Kicki's motion for a change of venue back was ultimately denied. Grifo said the defense was not able to prove that members of the jury would be prejudiced by the pretrial publicity.

This push for a venue change was a sign of a shift in strategy for the judge. His wife said he first dismissed this tactic when it was originally suggested by Glass. O'Kicki thought he would have the best chance of beating the charges in Cambria County because the people there knew him best.

With proceedings barreling toward a jury trial, Glass and Weaver advised the judge to seek a plea bargain deal that would allow him to keep his pension. O'Kicki and his wife would have none of it.

Glass and Weaver were fired.

———

As SUMMER FADED INTO fall in 1989, O'Kicki was feverishly at work on his case. He hired Richard Galloway, a prominent criminal-defense lawyer from Greensburg, and James Yelovich, the former district attorney of neighboring Somerset County. Their goal was to move the judge from the defensive to the offensive.

As his trial began, O'Kicki and his team claimed he'd been set up. He was, they said, a victim and scapegoat. Someone had abused his or her power to bring the crushing heel of state police down on the poor judge.

They laid the blame for this conspiracy at the foot of a Cambria County millionaire who, according to the judge, palled around with Mafia bosses and held the puppet strings of numerous politicians—including a Delaware senator who later became president of the United States.

Chapter 7

THE KINGMAKER

Somerset attorney George B. Kaufman hasn't forgotten his brief encounters with Wilbur E. Schonek, aka "Wid."

In the early 1980s, Kaufman was an election committee member for Somerset County Court of Common Pleas judge Norman A. Shaulis. He wanted to help Shaulis win his retention vote, so he and some others contacted management of Four Seasons Resort outside Jennerstown.

The resort—which included a rustic-looking clubhouse, pavilions, an indoor swimming pool, batting cages, a driving range and a nine-hole par-three golf course—was owned by Schonek, a resident of the Westmont community in neighboring Cambria County. Kaufman and his committee made arrangements to rent the resort from Schonek for their get-out-the-vote event.

"Several hundred people attended. One of my recollections of the picnic was Wid Schonek did attend the picnic," Kaufman said. "And he brought Joe Biden. We were introduced to him."

For Kaufman, the experience represented a brief glimpse at a different world. Millionaire powerbrokers who schmoozed with presidential hopefuls on private jets didn't routinely run in his social circles. He was a Republican assistant district attorney working in a rural county that leaned economically on agriculture and coal mining.

"I think he liked to play politics," Kaufman said of Schonek, "and he financially supported candidates that he liked."

Schonek was born on August 27, 1913. He was, not unlike O'Kicki, a self-made man. When his father died, Schonek was just sixteen years old. This meant it was time to work. By day, he found employment in public relations; at night, he helped out at a Johnstown auto parts store, eventually going full time and becoming the general manager. He left the store at the age of twenty-one to go into business for himself, stating that he wanted to avoid competing with the owner's family for promotions.

Schonek opened his first Dick's Auto Parts in the 1930s, and his company expanded vastly into a chain over the next fifty years, with branches opening in Delaware, West Virginia and Florida. Schonek also dabbled in other industries, operating the W.E. Schonek Insurance Agency in Johnstown's West End neighborhood and operating several television and radio stations in Florida dating back to 1957.

He was, by the mid-1900s, part of America's new-money set, a man who wielded tremendous power and influence. His charitable ventures included a 1982 campaign to renovate the Johnstown Incline Plane. He and his brother, R.C. "Boots" Schonek, pledged to donate $35,000 toward a required $50,000 match for $1.5 million in state and federal grants.

Primarily, however, Schonek was regarded as a kingmaker. Cambria County president judge Norman A. Krumenacker III acknowledged the local businessman's quiet role in politics. "[O'Kicki] knew Wid Schonek....I knew Wid Schonek, a lot of us knew [him]," Krumenacker said.

"Wid was always involved in politics and things like that. He was one of those behind-the-scenes-politician-type people. He would support people."

Recorded history of Schonek's political ventures spans the decades of recent history. The *Pittsburgh Press* reported in 1972 that Schonek had supported candidates from both major parties in an attempt to oust state senator Louis Coppersmith, a Johnstown Democrat. Coppersmith retaliated, according to Schonek, by demanding that Republican governor Milton Shapp remove Schonek from the commonwealth's Harness Racing Commission in exchange for Coppersmith's vote on a budget bill. Coppersmith denied having direct involvement but acknowledged that he was happy to see Schonek removed from the commission.

Schonek may have wanted to return the favor when he helped Mark Singel, the husband of Schonek's daughter Jackie, challenge Coppersmith for his seat in 1980. A September fundraiser for Singel made headlines in the *Daily American* newspaper that fall when Cambria County assistant district attorney John J. Kuzmiak was charged with "slugging" Paul Malinowsky, a Democratic mayoral candidate in Johnstown, during a Four Seasons soiree. The "slugfest" landed Malinowsky at Lee Hospital in Johnstown. He later dropped the charges, as "both parties expressed their sorrow that the incident had ever taken place," according to a press release from the Somerset County District Attorney's Office.

In the political fisticuffs, it was Schonek-backed Singel who emerged triumphant over Coppersmith. By the time of the O'Kicki trial several years later, Schonek's son-in-law had risen to the position of Pennsylvania lieutenant governor under Governor Robert Casey. Schonek, oddly enough, criticized Singel for the move. He characterized lieutenant governor as a "dead-end job" and claimed to have given Singel no help in that bid.

In other instances, however, Schonek was quick to take credit for political ascendancies. He discussed his hobby as kingmaker with the *Pittsburgh Press* in 1989 at the Johnstown–Cambria County Airport, the spot where he ate his lunch daily. Schonek talked about using his private plane to ferry politicians, including the late Pennsylvania state senator Hugh Scott and former Arizona senator Barry Goldwater, GOP nominee for the U.S. presidency in 1964. He bragged that his Four Seasons parties and fundraisers drew hundreds of prominent guests from across the business community and political sphere. Biden was mentioned as one of the many "national political figures" to attend his events.

"What I do is I guess you could call dabbling in politics," Schonek said at the time. "I don't smoke. I don't drink. I don't gamble. Politics is a great hobby for me.

"I don't contribute any money. You'll never see my name on a financial disclosure form. I'll tell you if I'm going to be with you and not just say it and then go behind your back to work for somebody else."

Schonek claimed that he supported O'Kicki when he ran for the bench in 1971, and his ties to the judge came under scrutiny as the judge and his attorneys went on the offensive at trial. Former *Johnstown Tribune-Democrat* editor George Fattman said he always felt that Schonek operated independently of the Democratic and Republican Parties.

"One thing that O'Kicki and Schonek may have had in common was that they both ran against the political grain. Schonek was always at outs with the Republican Party in Cambria County, which was headed by the Gleason family," Fattman said.

"I'm not sure what party affiliation O'Kicki did or did not have, but he ran against the grain also. So they might have…had that in common."

The *Pittsburgh Press* article—written in the midst of the O'Kicki trial—describes Schonek as a thick-built, pot-bellied man with the look of a steelworker, "his white hair in a close crewcut, his face…dominated by a bulbous nose" and his voice booming out in short, gravelly barks. Schonek acknowledged supporting O'Kicki's judicial run and claimed to have given the judge money on multiple occasions when he'd show up pouting about his financial problems and potentially having to dis-enroll his daughters from college.

"I gave [money] to him because I'm stupid," said Schonek, characterizing himself as "just some dumb Dutchman" in rich contrast to his high-profile persona. "There's nobody I gave more money than Judge O'Kicki, and I never expected to get it back. And now he claims I did this to him. Jeez."

Though O'Kicki denied receiving Schonek's help when he ran for judge, he acknowledged accepting money from the millionaire to put his children through college. O'Kicki later wrote:

I borrowed in 1981 the sum of $12,000 from U.S. Bank and $10,000 from Laurel National Bank in order to help finance the education of my other daughters. I was about 10 minutes to start court and Dick Green was one of the parties in waiting. I showed him my loan papers and asked how he was financing the medical education of his son. [Green said] "Wid and Boots [Rudolph] help and they don't charge interest. It is wrong for you to go to the banks; they talk too much about your personal business."…
About a week later I received a phone call from Dick Green that Wid wanted to meet me for lunch at the Johnstown airport. I attended. Wid told me [that] he would lend money to me at no interest and that I should repay his brother "Boots" whenever I had the money. He said he would hire two of the girls to do investigative work for some of his 26 stores. [It] sounded fine to me since in three months I was anticipating another tuition payment. Two days later Dick Green came to my office with two checks, each in the amount of $7,500. I took them home and had [daughters] Caroline and Joan endorse them and deposited them in my bank account. Boots came to my home that Saturday and he had two judgment notes—one for daughter Joan and me to sign in the amount of $6,000 and one for daughter Caroline and me to sign for a like amount, [payable] to Boots and his wife Gerry.
Boots said that Wid had further instructions for me. On [the] very next Saturday I called Wid at his Eisenhower Blvd office and asked if I could come and see him. Within ten minutes I received the "further instructions." From each $7,500 check I had to return $1,500 in cash to Wid, who said "how else can I finance campaigns of our friends." In addition, he asked that my two daughters do security checks on his personnel. He told me to select a product and go to each store and buy the product at five minutes

before lunchtime or closing time. Try to leave the money on the counter and don't wait for change. If the employee doesn't ring up the sale or give a receipt, then make a note of it. I accompanied Caroline and Joan as they visited 16 stores in Pa, Md and W. Va. during the summer of 1982. We bought a gallon of windshield wiper fluid at each store, varying in price from 79 cents to $2.29. The girls made a full report and I handed it to Wid around Thanksgiving time, jokingly saying that we were willing to survey the Florida stores over the Christmas holidays.

Connections between O'Kicki, Schonek and, to a lesser extent, Biden were recorded in yellow notepads used by O'Kicki's secretary to relay messages and keep track of the judge's phone calls. O'Kicki's widow, Sylvia Onusic, held on to a trove of these notepads and other documents from the judge over the decades.

For several years, the judge's meetings with Schonek were regular, if not daily. One of the secretary's notes, likely from 1986, contains a playful threat from the millionaire: "Wid Schonek…Waited for you for lunch yesterday. If you don't show up today, you buy next time. Wants you to call him."

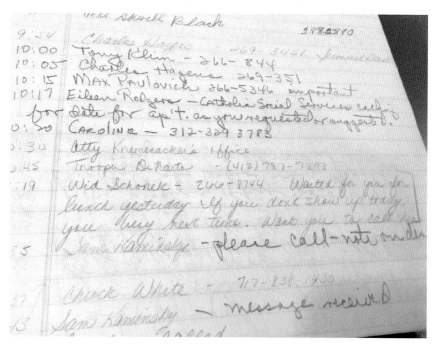

A 1980s note from Judge Joseph O'Kicki's secretary mentions that Wid Schonek called. "Waited for you for lunch yesterday," she relayed from Schonek. "If you don't show up today, you buy next time." *Photo by Bruce Siwy/*Daily American.

The origin of Schonek's relationship with the future U.S. president isn't spelled out, at least not in any of O'Kicki's materials. But in *The Bidens: Inside the First Family's Fifty-Year Rise to Power*, journalist Ben Schreckinger notes that Biden's law school buddy Jack Owens was an aide to Shapp. Owens convinced Shapp, a fellow Democrat, to campaign for Biden at an event in Wilmington, Delaware, when Biden first ran for U.S. Senate. Biden repaid Shapp by calling him "one of the most qualified men to be president" when the Pennsylvania governor announced that he was setting his sights on the White House in 1975. Shapp's longshot bid, however, swiftly deflated, and Biden switched his support to Jimmy Carter, the eventual winner of both the Democratic nomination and presidency.

Schonek, too, was wired in with Shapp. It was Shapp who had appointed Schonek, even though he was a Republican, to the Harness Racing Commission in 1971 after Schonek had supported Shapp's gubernatorial campaign.

It's conceivable, then, that Biden and Schonek met through their mutual friend, the governor.

According to Onusic, her husband's alliance with Schonek was an uneasy one. She said O'Kicki had a healthy fear of the man for his wealth and connections.

O'Kicki, during a televised post-trial interview, put it this way:

> *Mr. Schonek is involved in the political manipulation of county government. Mr. Schonek has a brother involved in the auto parts business with him by the name of Rudolph "Boots" Schonek. Rudolph "Boots" Schonek, on his own accord, made a gift of stock of Dick's Automotive to St. Francis College in late 1986. In March of 1987 Wid Schonek told me that he would cut off my head and stick it up my rear end for coercing his brother into giving money to a Catholic college. From that day on the investigation of Joe O'Kicki began.*
>
> *The various people that he had recommended for hiring in county government suddenly turned on me. These include Anthony Trigona, George Koban, Betty Krisko and Brenda Nasser. And, of course, Dick Green. Those are the major culprits who testified against me.*

Schonek, in his portion of the television segment, responded to the "chop off my head and stick it up my rear" comment: "No, I didn't say that. But let me say this: As big as his head was at the time you couldn't get it up an elephant's."

U.S. senator Joe Biden (D-Delaware) speaking with reporters about a congressional crime bill in 1994. *Library of Congress.*

Green—a former Republican senator who worked as Schonek's longtime personal attorney—was indeed among those who provided key testimony to state police. He alleged that O'Kicki had tried to extort a kickback from him after awarding a settlement to Green's client.

Green was interviewed by Rick Kirkham of *Inside Edition* in 1990. Green essentially admitted that Schonek was feeding information to state police.

> *Kirkham: "Has Mr. Schonek led you to believe he was out to get the judge?"*
> *Green: "Oh, he hates him. [Chuckles.] There's no doubt about it, he hates him."*
> *Kirkham: "Is Mr. Schonek, W.E. Schonek, behind an 'out-to-get-the-judge' campaign? Is that what brought Judge O'Kicki down?"*
> *Green: "[You can't] pull it out of thin air and say, 'Hey, he's not guilty because Wid Schonek started the investigation that produced the evidence.' It's the evidence that counts, the facts of the matter that count, not who started it."*

In an effort to counteract the negative and sometimes humiliating publicity generated by the trial and its proceedings, O'Kicki and allies bought a four-page newspaper insert. This insert was sponsored by a group calling itself the Committee for Justice for Judge Joseph F. O'Kicki. Robert Sutt was listed as chairman.

Leading off with the words "The TRUTH for Cambria County!" as its masthead, the publication had the style, tone and appearance of a tabloid. O'Kicki is described as a coal miner, a steelworker, a teacher and a professor—a "Man of the People!" It states that the judge had been framed and contains a letter that O'Kicki wrote to the *Wall Street Journal* in response to the newspaper's questions.

> *I don't know right now whose toes I've stepped on. I'll find out, eventually, who pushed the state police buttons into action.*
>
> *In Cambria County there are four major political factions: Democratic party ([William] Joseph), Republican party (Gleasons), Persio faction, and the Wilbur "Wid" Schonek forces. With the decline of political patronage coupled with the increase in the number of jobs covered by civil service or union agreements, the political power brokers such as Persio and Schonek have a strong voice in governmental affairs. The Persio faction usually fights within the Democratic party organization while the Schonek group battles in both camps.*

Despite stating that he didn't know "who pushed the state police buttons" earlier in his letter, O'Kicki went on to identify Schonek as the source of his troubles. He noted that he got along with the Joseph and Gleason groups and had ignored the Persio faction.

"It has now become the popular expedient, political ploy to attack judges. (Remember when all Americans of Slav descent were communists in the McCarthy era of early 50's; all Italians were mafia during the Costello era of the late 50's, etc.)," O'Kicki wrote.

"Just 60 years ago in Germany and Italy, those governments unleashed police power against its citizens. And the rest of the world, including responsible persons within those [countries], did nothing to stop it."

O'Kicki and his defense team were adamant that most of the heaviest charges against the judge were drummed up by Schonek's political cronies. They argued that key testimony was unreliable because it came almost exclusively from people close to an influential millionaire who had soured on O'Kicki a year before state police were tipped off to investigate the judge over unsubstantiated illegal gambling allegations.

The question was whether, and to what extent, the jurors would buy it.

Chapter 8

(MIS)TRIAL AND ERROR

On November 7, 1989, suspended Cambria County president judge Joseph F. O'Kicki stood trial at last in the Cambria County Courthouse he had once presided over. The eyes of the press and television, both local and national, were on the county seat of Ebensburg. Spokesman Robert Gentzel for the Pennsylvania attorney general characterized the case as one of the most closely watched in the history of his office.

Conspicuously absent—at least physically—from proceedings were several members of his family. Theresa, his first wife, did not attend. The *Philadelphia Inquirer* reported that their 1986 divorce had been bitter, the court records sealed. The seven O'Kicki daughters, also estranged, stayed away. And O'Kicki's mother, Antonia, died in November 1989 before the trial's conclusion.

O'Kicki maintained that he was innocent and would accept nothing short of exoneration. The initial seventy-six counts against him had been whittled down to twenty-seven. A total of ten were being heard in the public corruption trial. More than a dozen others were to be heard in a separate private corruption trial to be held at a later date.

In town for the proceedings, a *Philadelphia Inquirer* reporter described vividly the courtroom styles of both the new defense team and chief prosecutor. Regarding O'Kicki attorneys James Yelovich and Richard Galloway:

> [They] *have been vigorously attacking the credibility of the prosecution's witnesses. They have destroyed a few. One veteran court observer likens Yelovich to a cobra: He sways hypnotically in front of a witness, then strikes.*

Galloway, who wears a gold bracelet, goes for grander gestures, striding across the courtroom with terrific force and hurling questions in a sonorous tone. He likes to turn his back on the witness and stand foursquare before the jury. Sometimes, alone in the well of the court, he will peer aloft, leaving the witness' answer nowhere to fall except on Galloway's expressive face.

Deputy Attorney General Lawrence Claus was characterized as having a much different approach. Reporter Katharine Seelye wrote:

Low-key and methodical, Claus is building his case bit by bit. He is reserved in court, directing most of his questions from the prosecutor's table and marking his yellow legal pad as he makes each point. In contrast to the more free-wheeling defense attorneys, who frequently jangle the change in their trouser pockets, Claus tends to stand with one wrist pressed to the small of his back, military style. He rarely looks at the jury.

Looking back on the case, Claus said O'Kicki had acted routinely with brazen disregard for the law.

One of the things that was astounding to me—we had documentary evidence. We had, for example the...Laurel Bank letter. When we subpoenaed through the grand jury certain documents and found the document with the judge's letterhead with the secretary's initials who ultimately said, "Yeah, that was dictated to me by Joseph O'Kicki." And it basically covered all the elements of a classic bribery charge.

We knew that he didn't worry about things because he reduced that to writing and sent it out to one of the officials of the bank, in essence saying, "If you don't do what I want, don't bring your estate's trust case into my courtroom." Well, you just can't have that happen.

During the course of the trial, more than seventy-six witnesses were called to testify. O'Kicki was depicted as a "keen courtroom observer and an active participant in his defense." He took frequent notes on his legal pad and later gave more than ten hours of testimony over two days, disputing the allegations against him. The Associated Press reported that the judge wore a dark blue suit and dark tie embroidered with both his initials and the scales of justice.

Regarding the allegation that Interstate Fuels business partners bribed the judge for a favorable zoning decision on their strip-mining operation,

Anthony Capretti testified that he gave fellow co-owner Frank J. Romani $3,000. He stated that he asked Romani what happened to the cash a few months later.

"He said, 'I took care of the judge,'" Capretti said.

During cross-examination from Yelovich, Capretti admitted that he heard "street talk" years later that Romani never passed the money along to O'Kicki. He also stated that Romani never identified the judge in question by name and that he never pressed him for answers because the situation frightened him.

Romani, by the time of the trial, was serving a ten-year prison sentence after being convicted earlier that year on cocaine-trafficking charges.

In closing his argument on December 14, 1989, Yelovich hit back at the prosecution over the period of an hour and forty-five minutes. A victim, he told the jury, will typically go to the police. In this case, however, "the police have gone looking for the victims," according to the wishes of Schonek. He lambasted the investigation as taking a "barnyard" approach ("If you throw enough manure against the side of the barn, some of it will stick") and accused four former O'Kicki aides of being ingrates.

Brenda Nasser, one of two women to accuse the judge of sexual harassment, was characterized by Yelovich as an untrustworthy witness. He pointed to testimony that Nasser had sex with Schonek in his office and stated that she "flat-out lied" when she argued that this had never occurred.

Betty Krisko, another O'Kicki accuser, was given similar treatment. Yelovich noted that she had suffered a brain tumor, which should "cast doubt on what she saw."

The approach by the defense seemed, at least to some extent, effective. Claus acknowledged that his witnesses weren't always on the same page. An example was when former tipstaff George Koban said he gave Nasser $500 to give to the judge in order to secure a promotion within Cambria County government. Nasser testified that she had never accepted money for that reason.

"But those inconsistencies are not sufficient to negate proof of reasonable doubt of the crime," Claus said during his seventy-minute rebuttal. "The bottom line is, the money went to the judge."

"This case is not about rhetoric. It's about evidence. This man, Joseph O'Kicki...violated the very essence of his official responsibility and abused the power and abused the authority that you, the citizens of Cambria County, gave to him when you elected him."

For nearly seventeen hours, members of the jury deliberated on O'Kicki's fate.

Ebensburg attorney Tim Burns said in retrospect:

> *Did Judge O'Kicki get a fair trial? You know, it's hard for me to say that. And the reason is, he wasn't convicted on all counts. So that means that the jury did talk about it, you know, they didn't go in there—a half hour later, boom, "He's guilty."*
>
> *So do I feel the jury pool was appropriate? No. But at the same time, it's hard for me to say he didn't get a fair trial since they did debate.*

Of the ten charges he faced at this juncture, O'Kicki was found guilty of six. His convictions included bribery, coercion, official oppression and demanding money for a promotion. Members of the jury decided that the judge had solicited a bribe from attorney Dick Green after increasing his client's settlement from $140,000 to $240,000. They also convicted O'Kicki of soliciting a $500 loan from Green and another $500 payment from a former tipstaff seeking a higher-paying job with the county.

O'Kicki was found not guilty of open lewdness, as accused by former secretaries, and counts related to seeking strip-mining kickbacks from cocaine trafficker Romani, as alleged by former tipstaff Tony Trigona.

According to the *Morning Call* newspaper, even the jury's findings were not without drama of their own. One of the jurors, when asked to state his verdicts, said "not guilty" on some of the counts that the jury foreman said were unanimous. This led the defense to argue for a mistrial.

Burns characterized this as a wild and unusual twist to the proceedings. "The jury was not unanimous. In a criminal trial you have to be unanimous, but the second judge bypassed that," he said. "I mean, if the jury was not unanimous, it should have been a mistrial or new trial. So that really surprised me that there's allegations made that it wasn't a unanimous verdict."

Claus, unsurprisingly, disagreed with the mistrial argument. He noted that the foreman's verdict slip and the verdict slips filled out by each juror were identical. This, he said, was evidence that the decisions were unanimous.

Judge Grifo agreed.

And so O'Kicki was cooked. The man sworn in as the county's president judge less than two years prior was now a convict. He would be stripped of his $80,000 salary and pension. His sentence could include a maximum of twenty-six years.

Ironically, O'Kicki would never serve even a day in jail.

Instead, Attorney General Ernest Preate—whose office prosecuted the judge—would himself end up in federal prison.

Chapter 9

"I'LL BE HOME FOR CHRISTMAS"

T hree years after her husband's trial, Sylvia Onusic was settling into life in Ljubljana, Slovenia.

Intrigued by public health and nutrition topics, she entered the fledgling central European nation as a student on a Fulbright Scholarship. She was also a teacher of sorts: one of her two young sons was of the potty-training age. Onusic said she tried to inspire him to use the toilet like a big kid by telling him that Santa Claus might bring his father for Christmas if he ditched the diapers.

On December 8, 1992, the little boy took this encouragement to heart and used the bathroom for his business. A short time later, a knock came at their door.

Arriving in Ljubljana just in time for the holiday season was the boy's father, renowned American jurist—and soon-to-be international fugitive—Joseph F. O'Kicki.

ON THE HEELS OF his widely publicized trial, O'Kicki faced a new set of challenges. He had already gone to the hospital on August 15, 1988, for acute hypertension and heart arrhythmia. He was again hospitalized in March and September of 1989 and in February 1991 underwent bypass

Traffic flowing through the streets of Ljubljana, Slovenia. *Courtesy of Tim Burns.*

surgery following a heart attack. His attorney said he suffered from partially blocked arteries and high blood pressure. Doctors diagnosed him with Dressler's syndrome, a condition that causes a fluid buildup that can result in congestive heart failure. Physician Sheo Shrivastava told Judge Richard Grifo, "Death would not be an unexpected result" if O'Kicki was forced to stand trial in the summer of 1991.

Grifo agreed to reschedule O'Kicki's second trial for January 1992. The judge still faced sixteen charges of fraud, conspiracy and corruption related to allegations from the 1989 grand jury presentment. The second trial was delayed again, this time indefinitely, as the appeal of his original convictions moved from state Superior Court to the state Supreme Court.

Medical problems would continue to pile up for the judge. He was diagnosed with cancer and had surgery for it in January 1992. In January 1993, he reported falling and breaking his wrist in two places.

As O'Kicki moved to postpone his legal challenges to deal with health concerns, prosecutors moved to halt his pay. O'Kicki continued to receive checks of approximately $3,100 every two weeks. The commonwealth's Judicial Inquiry and Review Board requested action from the Pennsylvania Supreme Court, but the justices seemed in no hurry to address the situation. This prompted Attorney General Ernest Preate to ask the state treasurer to stop O'Kicki's payments in April 1991, stating at a press conference that the judge "shouldn't be at the public trough, taking money as a convicted felon for doing absolutely nothing." Additional pressure came from the Washington Legal Foundation, a national public-interest law group, which opined that O'Kicki's state paychecks were a "slap in the face to already overburdened Pennsylvania taxpayers."

Just a few weeks later, the commonwealth complied. Counsel for Pennsylvania treasurer Catherine Baker Knoll said O'Kicki would no longer receive checks unless the Administrative Office for Pennsylvania Courts provided written justification for why the judge should receive his salary.

"I haven't even had the courtesy to get a copy of the letter Preate sent to Knoll," O'Kicki said of the situation. "But we do plan legal action.

"We're so close to getting this whole thing resolved that this is just a waste of money. This whole thing is a publicity device for state Attorney General Preate."

The Pennsylvania Supreme Court disagreed. Justices sided with Knoll in reaffirming that O'Kicki should not receive his $80,000 annual salary amid his suspension.

They stopped short, however, of removing the judge from office. Their ruling stated that O'Kicki could keep his title at least until his appeals process had played out.

At the advice of his attorneys, O'Kicki had been somewhat quiet during his widely publicized public corruption trial. That began to change after he was sentenced in June 1990 to serve two to five years in prison.

Instead of shirking silently into obscurity, O'Kicki began what might be characterized as a bizarre public relations campaign. He filed suit in January 1991 in U.S. District Court against the *Wall Street Journal*, reporter Milo Geyelin and Warren H. Phillips, CEO of the newspaper's parent company, Dow Jones. The judge said that he warned Geyelin that the information he intended to publish was false and that Geyelin and the *Wall Street Journal* printed it anyway in its November 1, 1989 edition. O'Kicki claimed that the article caused "severe and irreparable damage to his economic status and his personal and professional reputation in the community and throughout the United States." The suit did not, however, specify what he thought the newspaper had gotten wrong.

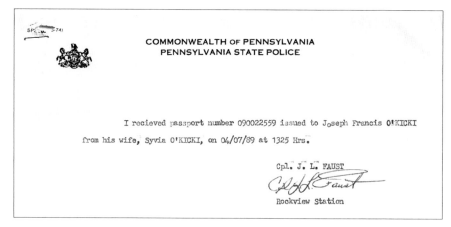

This memo from Pennsylvania State Police corporal J.L. Faust states that Joe O'Kicki's wife surrendered his passport on April 7, 1989. *Courtesy of Sylvia Onusic.*

O'Kicki also began to give more interviews to media both local and national. The ex-judge told a reporter with local news channel WWCP TV that he still felt supported by many people in Cambria County.

"Those for whom I have done the most are the ones that have run the farthest," O'Kicki said. "Those ordinary people who know me for what I am come up to shake my hand...and wish me luck and wish me well."

In a March 1990 edition of the *Altoona Mirror*, O'Kicki described his post-conviction mindset: "Empty. Disillusionment...very shocked to find injustice—not having justice administered to me when I need it most."

He expressed some optimism as well, in spite of his circumstance. "The truth," O'Kicki said, "will prevail....The truth will set me free."

Maybe O'Kicki was banking on the truth. But what set him free was a cunning backup plan.

According to a state police record, Onusic surrendered O'Kicki's passport on April 7, 1989. Yet he made two trips to Slovenia after this occurred: the first in the winter of 1992 and the second in the spring of 1993.

Onusic said:

> He went to Canada, he flew to Germany, he rented a car and he drove down to Slovenia. He had the car...and then I guess he returned it. It was a rental car.
>
> But I found his notes just lately about what cars he was going to rent, where he was going to rent, where he was going to go to get the tickets and everything. Nobody reported...who sold him the tickets. It was a State College travel agency—a friend of ours sold him the tickets. And I talked to this friend and I said, "I'm so sorry, I hope you didn't have any problems when the police came to see you." And he goes, "Oh, heck no, I got so much business over that, I want to thank you for doing that."

O'Kicki's first journey to Slovenia was apparently undetected by authorities. He was able to visit his family for several weeks before returning to America without triggering an arrest or a word in the press.

Per Onusic: "There was the storm of the century....Somehow somebody got word to him or me that [at] one of his buildings, the roof had fallen down. So he goes, 'You know, I'd better really go back 'cause all my papers are probably flying all over the neighborhood and it's going to be a mess and everything.' So then on the 14th of January he went back. He went back through Toronto...Frankfurt [to] Toronto."

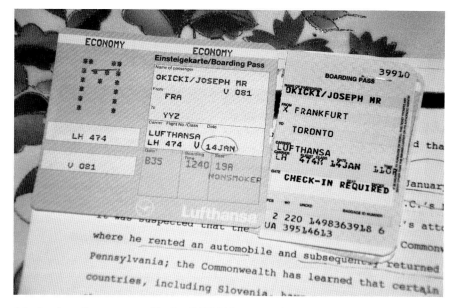

A look at boarding passes used by Joe O'Kicki for a secretive return flight from Europe to America in January 1993. *Photo by Eric Kieta/*Daily American.

The death blow to O'Kicki's dream of normalcy came just weeks later. Members of the Supreme Court of Pennsylvania concluded in late February 1993 that they would not hear the judge's appeal. Abstaining from the decision were Justices Stephen A. Zappala and John P. Flaherty, the Supreme Court judge who had showered O'Kicki with praise during his swearing-in celebration less than five years prior.

Preate told the *Post-Gazette* he would motion to have O'Kicki's bail revoked so the judge could begin his jail sentence. Defense attorneys, meanwhile, indicated that additional appeals could be coming, including a petition to federal court.

But in declining his case, the Supreme Court cemented O'Kicki's alternate plans. On March 3, 1993, Deputy Attorney General Lawrence Claus filed a motion asking for the judge to be jailed. He speculated that O'Kicki may be en route to Slovenia. Five days later, both O'Kicki and his legal defense were absent for a court hearing in Easton. Claus told Grifo that O'Kicki had called his lawyer a few days prior to say he had been hospitalized again but didn't say where he was staying.

Grifo had heard enough. He revoked the bond, and law enforcement across the country was put on alert via computerized networks to look for the "aging, white-bearded" judge.

Preate declared that "O'Kicki is to be arrested on sight."

The search was on. Police scoured hospitals across western Pennsylvania. Interpol, the European police network tasked with finding convicts, was alerted. Prosecutors noted that the judge's wife and youngest children lived in Slovenia.

Arthur Cohen, a Hollidaysburg attorney, said O'Kicki had eaten at his house on March 1, a week prior to the skipped hearing. He added that he thought the judge was heading to State College. He didn't say why.

Compounding the confusion was the fact that O'Kicki's wife—who had legally changed her last name to Onusic two years prior—was filing for divorce. The petition arrived in Centre County from Slovenia on March 10.

O'Kicki continued to call his attorney, James Yelovich, claiming he was in the hospital. He remained coy about where this hospital was located and made no indication that he was planning to turn himself in.

"I don't think he cares much," Yelovich said. "I think he's sick."

An "O'Kicki sighting" was also reported in State College on March 10. A caller told Cambria County sheriff Jay Roberts that he tailed a man who looked like the judge for approximately two blocks and then followed him into a post office so he could hear his voice. The supposed witness said he recognized the judge because O'Kicki had been in town a few weeks earlier to buy and mail some books to his wife and had sought "bogus receipts so he could get the books through customs at a cheaper cost."

"Once he heard the voice, he was convinced it was O'Kicki and went out to the nearest pay phone to call the police," Roberts said. "The State College police are 95 percent sure this is an official sighting."

"O'Kicki likes to control the situation," Roberts added. "It wouldn't surprise me if he is sitting under everybody's nose and watching all this unfold."

Neil Price, an attorney from Johnstown who assisted O'Kicki on occasion, was much closer to the mark. He tellingly revealed some advice he'd given the judge when he learned of O'Kicki's cancer diagnosis: "I told him he should leave the country."

The judge had done just that. O'Kicki was putting the United States, his two- to five-year sentence and $300,000 tab for fines, costs and restitution into the rearview.

"He knew he wouldn't get justice," Onusic said. "He had heard the Supreme Court had refused to hear his appeal, so on the second of March, he flew from Toronto to Munich and then the next day he came to Ljubljana."

Authorities eventually caught on. Roberts told the *Philadelphia Inquirer* that authorities traced these airline ticket purchases to the judge and confirmed that someone had used them. He said they also discovered that O'Kicki had shipped his red 1984 Pontiac Sunbird from Baltimore to Bremerhaven, Germany, back in November. Additional credit card purchases were made in late February at spots in Buffalo and Connecticut, a move that investigators characterized as a ploy to make them believe he was remaining in the country.

"The paper chase goes on," Roberts said.

Onusic herself played a role in the obfuscation of her husband's whereabouts. Tony Palm, a friend of the judge's who worked as a Johnstown-area police officer, said O'Kicki's wife called him on March 20 to ask about developments in America and request that he keep an eye on their home.

When Palm told her that police had released info about the judge flying to Europe during the first week of the month, "She said, 'They don't know what they're talking about.'"

As time passed, speculation grew more rampant. Roberts put it thusly in late March: "We know he's going to be seen more than Elvis in the next couple of weeks. He'll be seen more than Elvis and Jimmy Hoffa."

William Keisling, an author who wrote about corruption in Pennsylvania, acknowledged that he'd been corresponding with O'Kicki via fax, phone and mail. The judge updated Keisling on his health and hinted at his plans, while stopping short of divulging his location, in a letter received by the author on April 3. O'Kicki wrote:

> *Yes I have colorectal cancer. I am partially incontinent, must be at the bathroom 6 to 10 times per day. Also, I have congestive heart failure, must take pills regularly to keep fluid from building up in my lungs. Was hospitalized and treated on Feb. 28, 1993 for right bundle branch blocking of the heart.*
>
> *But the real key is to get the Supreme Court to reconsider its order and grant the allocatur. The facts in our case are stronger than those in* Com. vs. Jay Smith, *the school principal recently freed from a murder rap. Keep in touch.*
>
> *Read the complaint, amended complaint, second amended complaint, and Rico statement filed in federal court in Johnstown no. 9169J.*
>
> *urgent that you read those papers as soon as possible. Joe.*

Thus began perhaps the wildest chapter of the O'Kicki saga. His traverse across eastern Europe was documented by *Pittsburgh Post-Gazette* journalist Dennis Roddy, who took to the road to sniff out the judge and send copy home to a news-hungry American readership. He reported that O'Kicki

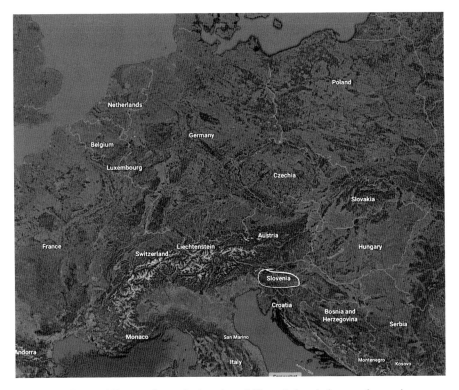

This map of central Europe shows the location of Slovenia in relation to other nations. *Courtesy of Google Earth.*

"changed his address, shaved his beard, arranged for a mail drop at his father's birthplace, and moved from spot to spot, sometimes begging for a place to stay" since he left the United States.

According to Roddy, a landlord in Lesce, Slovenia, had a sour experience with O'Kicki. Justina Globocnik said the fugitive judge pleaded for a break when she informed him that she needed a year's worth of rent up front. He told her that he and his two young sons would have to sleep in his car if she didn't work with him. Globocnik allowed him to stay there with just the first month's payment, but he swiftly wore out his welcome by tying up the telephone and bathroom and somehow convincing her to do his laundry for him. She soon asked him to leave.

"When we would say no to something, he would just push to get his way," Globocnik said, adding that he characterized himself as both a legal adviser and economics expert in separate conversations with her and her husband. "He was too pushy.

"He didn't pay his phone bill. He said he would pay his phone bill later."

Also part of the O'Kicki pilgrimage was a visit with family in Volckova Vas. He had been there twenty-three years prior to sign over a home from his mother, Antonia, to relative Pepsa Bucar. Marjan Medved, Bucar and other distant family members of the judge spoke well of him and invited him to stay there after the Easter holiday. He later called to decline.

As Roddy traced the judge's footsteps, it became increasingly clear that O'Kicki was skipping around Slovenia. This certainty, however, didn't bring authorities much closer to jailing the Johnstown judge.

Brian Sukenik, one of O'Kicki's longtime friends, remembered receiving an unexpected phone call approximately one year after the judge had fled the country. He said of the call:

> My mom goes, "It's for you." And I got on and he goes, "Hey, Brian, it's the judge." And…we chit-chatted for a while. I said, "Well, how's Slovenia?" He said, "Oh, I love it, I'm teaching, I'm doing this, I'm doing that."
>
> And I said, "Well, that's good.….Now, can you explain to me how you got out of the country since you had to forfeit your American passport?" And he says, "I'm not an American."

The revelation summed up the situation.

Because his parents had been citizens of present-day Slovenia, O'Kicki was eligible to live there. He applied for, and received, both a citizenship and passport from that nation before ever attempting to leave America.

"I was always under the impression that when you moved to United States, let's say, that you renounce your old citizenship and petition the government for citizenship here," said Walt Komoroski, one of the state troopers who had investigated O'Kicki. "Not sure what the dynamic was there. But he still had his Yugoslav [Slovenian] passport.

"We thought by taking his United States passport from him that we were…guaranteed his presence at the second trial. But nope."

Questions surfaced regarding why authorities hadn't brought O'Kicki back to America. This became the subject of a local WWCP-TV news segment. The chief of Slovenian national law enforcement told an American television reporter during the interview that no one from the FBI, Pennsylvania attorney general or Interpol had inquired about O'Kicki. He said the only extradition question they had received came from the deputy sheriff of Cambria County.

Slovenian authorities said that O'Kicki was safe from extradition because of his citizenship. They noted that, under their treaty with America, the judge could be forced to serve his sentence in Slovenia if his conviction held under Slovenian law.

He was never re-tried in Slovenia, perhaps because he was a nonviolent offender.

Far from life as a fugitive, O'Kicki settled into living in Ljubljana. He assimilated with Slovenian society and ended up working for its government. Onusic said Ljubljana mayor Dimitrij Rupel brought the ex-judge on as a consultant. O'Kicki found work also as a translator, public school teacher and private English instructor and as an employee of Gospodarski Vestnik, a large business publishing house in Slovenia. American consul to Slovenia David W. Ball told a reporter that O'Kicki, ever the hustler, won a bet against him regarding a Penn State–Ohio State football game. Ball was obliged to buy him lunch.

Overseas and apparently free from the threat of extradition and imprisonment, O'Kicki's health problems outweighed his legal concerns. His widow said he struggled with a cancer diagnosis and other ailments.

"I was always amazed by him because even though he was so sick, he had all these troubles, the state had taken away his…they had maneuvered, all the little soldiers had maneuvered to take away his disability, which he worked really hard for, take away his Social Security which he had paid into his whole life.…They took away his law license," Onusic said.

"[But] he still had the energy and will and drive to go out and work and contribute to the household."

Regarding the reason for his flight from America, Onusic said O'Kicki believed he'd be killed if he served time anywhere with members of the Outlaws gang, citing his 1980s sentencing of bikers convicted of assaulting police officers in Nanty Glo.

"When Judge Grifo sentenced him to jail, there was a story [about how] he's really afraid of jail. And I think Grifo intended to send him where the Outlaws were put," she said. "I don't know if that's true or not, but that's what I heard."

O'Kicki repeated his fears publicly as well.

"It's a death sentence for me to go to Western Penitentiary or any other state prison facility," he said in one televised interview. "Over the years I've sentenced many people to lengthy terms for rape or murder, for other serious offenses. These people are still in prison. These people have long memories. My chances of survival are between zero and nil.

"We don't have a prison system. It's a warehouse."

In addition to working various jobs in Slovenia, O'Kicki was doing some writing. His topic of choice was corruption in Pennsylvania. The judge was maintaining his innocence and compiling documentation about the people he believed had wronged or betrayed him. And he was bringing these allegations to federal authorities back in America.

"Someday, somehow, somewhere," he said, "I'll be back in Cambria County."

PART II

"THE FIX"

Chapter 10

THE DRO SCANDAL

Following the five frenzied years of ignominy, trial and fugitive flight, the circumstances surrounding the life of the infamous Slovenian denizen settled into something more routine. Joe O'Kicki worked various jobs in Slovenia. He continued to maintain his innocence, plead for a new trial and hurl accusations from overseas. An insidious attack by "the pigs, Arabs and Italians" had ended his career. His rants hit, among others, Cambria County judge Gerald Long, Clerk of Courts James McNulty, Ebensburg attorney Dino Persio, Johnstown businessman Frank Pasquerilla, western Pennsylvania developers Damian and George Zamias and Richard "Dick" Green.

O'Kicki would find at least some vindication in relation to the domestic relations office investigation he initiated as his opening salvo as president judge.

A few months after he was fired by Judge Caram Abood in the fall of 1988, Brian Sukenik was contacted by Trooper Robert M. Ando of Pennsylvania State Police. Sukenik had been rehired in the Ebensburg courthouse at O'Kicki's behest in the summer of that year to produce evidence of suspected corruption in Cambria County's domestic relations office.

"I was cooperating with the white-collar crime unit then because they were having problems with the expense accounts," Sukenik said. "There were a lot of fudged documents. People that travel in the same car together were writing two different expense accounts, then they'd go and get signed off on by Judge Abood and then they'd go down to the commissioner's office and they'd have checks faster than any other vendor around. And Ron Stephenson, I think, was the president commissioner."

His first sit-down with state police was nearly derailed when Sukenik saw that Trooper Walt Komoroski and Bill Russell had arrived. Sukenik knew them for their involvement in investigating O'Kicki. Sukenik said:

> *We met at Dean's Diner in Blairsville. Bob Ando was the officer-in-charge....And then the stooges showed up, Komoroski and Russell. And I flipped out....I said I don't need those two criminals anywhere near this. So you need to get 'em to go.*
>
> *He went back outside and talked to them, and they got in their car and they took off. They weren't happy, but I don't really care. So we sat back down and he ended up following us back to my house in up in Geistown and we sat there at the dining room table and started going over things.*

According to Sukenik, several in-house interrogations were later held at his home. He reviewed with police the memos, invoices, bank records and other documents in question from the county's domestic relations office. Sukenik estimated that these sessions lasted four to six hours each time.

A taste of some of Ljubljana's more colorful and ornate architecture. *Courtesy of Tim Burns.*

"Judge Abood said I'm an outright liar and I probably forged all those documents," Sukenik said, relaying what Ando had told him.

"We spent another couple hours, probably maybe six, seven hours total, going over all the paperwork and the forms and the invoices, and he was questioning me more....Some of the things they did...was just showing a pattern of hiding things."

Though Sukenik wanted to sue the county for wrongful termination, state police asked him to comply with a gag order and promise silence. He said they told him they would halt their investigation immediately if he discussed the matter. His final correspondence with state police about the situation took place in June 1990 when he received a subpoena to testify in court.

Less than a year later, on May 29, 1991, the *Altoona Mirror* reported that an independent audit of the Cambria County domestic relations office had finally been made public. The audit findings were damning: Barnes, Saly and Co. had discovered that the office spent an "excessive amount of money" on computer equipment and services from Ecco Consulting. Their report stated that more than $554,162 county tax dollars were paid to Ecco between 1983 and 1989. Approximately $467,601 was related to the original bid, even though that bid had been approved for just $206,305.

"We were unable to verify with any degree of certainty that the computer equipment which was paid for was actually received....We were unable to track the disposition of the old computer equipment," the report stated.

The *Mirror* noted that Regis Link, who managed the computer department for the domestic relations office, had cooperated in the state police investigation. He, like Sukenik and others, had been fired by Abood.

Coinciding with the release of the audit was Abood's abrupt resignation from the bench. He delivered a prepared statement from his Cambria County courtroom announcing that he had informed Governor Robert P. Casey and Supreme Court justice Robert N.C. Nix Jr. that he would be officially stepping down on July 7, 1991. His plans were to join a three-man law firm in Johnstown. "It is simply time for me to take a new direction in my life," he said.

The timing of the resignation was not lost on reporters. The former district attorney and judge of fifteen years was asked whether he was under investigation for malfeasance in the county's domestic relations office.

"In 15 and a half years that I have served as judge there has not, to my knowledge, been one complaint to the Judicial Inquiry Review Board about my service," Abood said. "[I am] leaving by the front door, not the back door."

The Barnes, Saly & Company findings were handed to Cambria County district attorney Timothy Creany. It's unclear whether anyone served jail time over the audit results.

O'Kicki made a point to gloat over the findings during a television interview before his 1993 escape to Slovenia.

"It's very blatant in that you have the county paying $24,600 for a contract to do a study and no study is ever made," O'Kicki said. "That's a clear blatant violation of law."

According to Sukenik, one of the red flags was that payments to Ecco were often just below $25,000. Spending of $25,000 or more, he said, required state approval.

Audit: Cambria agency spent beyond bid

By Linda Hudkins
Staff Writer

EBENSBURG — An audit indicating an excessive amount of money was spent on computer equipment for Cambria County's Domestic Relations Office during the 1980s has been given to the district attorney for investigation.

The independent audit, conducted by Barnes, Saly and Company of Johnstown, indicates the equipment was purchased from Ecco Consult

See Audit on Page B3

Mirror file photo

Caram Abood

Abood: Not fleeing probe

EBENSBURG — Cambria County's Acting President Judge Caram J. Abood said this morning he is resigning and "leaving by the front door, not the back door."

He said he will be joining a three-man Johnstown law firm which will be adding two partners.

In a prepared statement delivered at a press conference in his courtroom, the judge said he sent letters of resignation dated today to Gov.

See Abood on Page B3

News coverage of the Cambria County domestic relations office audit and abrupt resignation of Judge Caram Abood in May 1991. *Courtesy of the* Altoona Mirror.

"They didn't have anybody from the state reviewing it. So it was just too convenient," Sukenik said. "You know, it's like saying, 'That building's on fire, but I didn't set it' as I stood with my gallon of gasoline and matches."

Even as he remained a fugitive in Slovenia, O'Kicki attempted to sue Abood and law partner Richard "Dick" Green for a decades-old dispute about whether the pair had ever paid O'Kicki for the purchase of his law firm when he became judge. He accused former secretary Brenda Nasser of stealing their contract when he fired her in 1980, noting that she was represented by Green during the employment dispute. O'Kicki also motioned for Cambria County president judge Norman A. Krumenacker to recuse himself. He cited his involvement with the case as a conflict of interest, claiming that Krumenacker and his father supported Abood during his 1985 reelection campaign by financing a fundraiser organized by prominent businessmen George Zamias and Frank Pasquerilla at the North Fork Country Club.

The DRO affair, according to O'Kicki, was merely the tip of the iceberg. He had plenty more to say about the state of affairs in Cambria County and the Commonwealth of Pennsylvania. And he was writing a book on the subject.

Its tentative title was "The Fix."

Chapter 11

ERNIE THE ATTORNEY

When Joe O'Kicki wrote to U.S. attorney general Janet Reno on August 25, 1993, he opened with a mini treatise on the evolution of organized crime. What followed was a blitz of staggering accusations: banks colluding with mob bosses, judges fixing cases for the politically connected and police ignoring organized crime killings. O'Kicki ended his mini manifesto by asking Reno to reinstate his pension in exchange for his cooperation in lighting fire to the pervasive web of corruption in Cambria County and across the commonwealth.

"By the order of the Supreme Court, I was directed to 'clean up the system,'" O'Kicki told Reno, "but not long afterwards I was politically removed by suspension, arrest and conviction, in a campaign led by the attorney general to cower the independent judiciary in Pennsylvania.

"[Ernest Preate] has successfully continued with his campaign against the judiciary by abuse of prosecutorial powers through threats of investigation and prosecution, has virtual control over the functions of the superior and supreme courts. His power grows, unchallenged and unchecked. After all, who can prosecute him?"

This question—though likely rhetorical—would soon be answered.

"Oh, he's crazy," Preate told a reporter for the local Channel 8 television station in the early 1990s when questioned about whether he thought O'Kicki's insights would be useful toward future investigations. "You know, this a guy that's thumbed his nose at the law. He ought to know better. He ought to turn himself in and serve his time like a man.

"Certainly...I've never prevented him from presenting any evidence whatsoever, whether he wanted it to present before a grand jury or wanted to present it before the court itself when they heard his case when he had every opportunity to do it. If he didn't do it, that's his problem."

A reporter pressed on. If O'Kicki was part of the corruption, she asked, wouldn't he know a lot about it?

"I don't know what he knows," Preate said. "You can't talk to him if he's overseas. The guy's been a loony tune for the last couple of years."

The irritation from Preate was palpable. It's possible he knew what O'Kicki was writing about him to Reno or others.

From O'Kicki:

> *Presently in 1992 and still pending, Ernie Preate arrested, after many warnings that video poker machines were illegal and would be seized by the* [Pennsylvania] *state police, one of the largest video poker machine operators in Western Pennsylvania and charged him with organizing a gambling operation together with Judge* [Gerald] *Long's tipstaff* [Spiro Tsakalis, father of a Pennsylvania state trooper].*
>
> *While video poker machines were being seized by the Pa attorney general's office and the state police, the Tsakalis machines mostly escaped seizure. Bars and clubs in Northern Cambria County were forewarned by the prosecutor's office that the raid by the State Police was forthcoming.*

Substantive evidence for the judge's insinuation—that the commonwealth's chief law enforcement officer was complicit in a scheme to both cover for and profit from illegal gambling—is absent from his letter. But the fact is that Preate was indeed being hounded by these rumors.

In his book *We'll Make You an Offer You Can't Refuse*, former Pennsylvania Crime Commission executive director Frederick T. Martens laid out his case against the ex–attorney general. He explained how an investigation began when the United States attorney for the Middle District of Pennsylvania took some initial steps in 1990. The allegation was that Preate had extorted cash from illegal poker machine operators to help fund his campaign. One of those operators, Joseph Kovach, worked with the FBI to record incriminating conversations with others in the illegal gambling business that corroborated this claim. The case, however, appeared to die with Kovach, who passed away soon afterward. His death was attributed to natural causes.

In January 1992, the probe was given new oxygen when Kovach business partner Elmo Baldassari told Pennsylvania Crime Commission agents that the attorney general was in fact in his pocket. Baldassari was a well-known mob boss in northeastern Pennsylvania. He told the crime commission that he and others in the illegal gambling business had provided Preate with thousands in black-market profits. Baldassari was angry that Preate had not acted to help him when he went to prison for threatening the life of a man who owed him money.

Martens said they later obtained a copy of a check from a video poker operator in Erie to Preate's attorney general campaign. They found that $150,000 was unaccounted for after thorough review of Preate's campaign records.

"There's an old saying," Martens said during a recent interview. "'When you're sleeping with dogs, you get fleas.'"

Aware of the career-threatening investigation, Preate and allies in the Pennsylvania legislature began a public relations campaign of their own against the crime commission. This came to a vote in June 1994, and the outcome was overwhelming: the commission was abolished by a 44–3 vote in the Senate and 120–79 vote in the House.

Preate and friends had crushed the Pennsylvania Crime Commission but not the investigation. Crime commission findings were handed to newly appointed U.S. attorney David Barasch, who empaneled a federal grand jury.

A year later, on June 6, 1995, Preate pleaded guilty to mail fraud. The *New York Times* reported that he had accepted a plea agreement to avoid a trial and the indictment of his brothers Carlon and Robert.

At the sentencing in December 1995, Barasch said that Preate "lied to the public...about the scope of the contributions...and repeatedly misinformed the public throughout his tenure as Attorney General...continued to abuse a position of public trust up until his guilty plea...[that] he would use these campaign contributions to assist him in securing the office, title and position of the Attorney General of Pennsylvania....No citizen voted to have a felon as their chief law enforcement officer." Preate was then sentenced by the judge to fourteen months in prison, a $25,000 fine, two years' probation and three hundred community service hours.

For Preate—a Vietnam veteran and son of a prominent attorney who had served in the administration of Pennsylvania governor William Scranton—it was a dramatic fall from grace. He had been a favorite for governor at the time of the commission's investigation, losing a fairly close race to Tom Ridge in the Republican primary. Ridge would of course go on to become governor.

After serving his prison term and enduring a temporary suspension of his law license, Preate returned to the legal field. He remains a practicing attorney in Scranton.

Preate declined the opportunity for an extended interview about the O'Kicki case. He said he remembered little about the investigation but shared some personal thoughts about the late judge's swearing-in at the Cambria County Courthouse: "It was more like the coronation of a king than the swearing in of a president judge. That is my recollection—that he suffered from delusions of grandeur."

Before hanging up, Preate added, "Thanks for the memories, kid."

There's undeniable irony in the parallels between Preate, the attorney general, and O'Kicki, the judge. The career prosecutor had greenlighted the investigation of O'Kicki in 1988 for allegedly tipping off illegal gambling operators while Preate himself had taken money from mob racketeers for his attorney general campaign.

Was O'Kicki guilty of these illegal gambling ties?

"I don't know what the answer to that is, I really don't, because I wasn't involved with Troop A vice," said retired trooper Walt Komoroski, the lone surviving member of the duo who investigated the judge. "My roots are in criminal investigation."

The hypocrisy of Preate's office—and the lack of evidence that O'Kicki was tied to gambling interests, which was a pretext for the state police probe—wasn't lost on the exiled judge. Unable to convince a jury of his innocence, he worked to convince the general public of a more collective guilt, starting with his old nemesis.

"He was gathering information and he wrote a lot of letters," Onusic said. "He wrote so many things to his attorneys if I just gathered that into a book and edited it that would be 'The Fix.' Because he described to Janet Reno, he described to other people how things, cases were 'fixed' in Cambria County."

Chapter 12

"WID" AND "BOOTS"

In a roster labeled "The Players" amid his notes and manuscripts, Joe O'Kicki placed Wilbur "Wid" Schonek atop a pyramid of supposed political underlings. O'Kicki claimed that Schonek was the "financial godfather" of influential figures on both the national and local scales: U.S. senator Joe Biden, U.S. senator Arlen Specter, Johnstown mayor Herb Pfuhl, Cambria County commissioners Ron Stephenson and Joseph Roberts, Cambria County district attorney Tim Creany, county judges Caram Abood and Gerry Long and at least three district magistrates. He rounded out Schonek's team with retired IRS auditor Anthony Klim and Richard "Dick" Green, the former state senator who served as legal counsel for the City of Johnstown. O'Kicki called Green the "Personal Solicitor and daily luncheon companion" of Schonek, alleging that 20 percent of his annual fees came from Schonek.

"Each player contributes his expertise to accomplish many illegal purposes," O'Kicki said. "Green utilizes his legal skills to form the corporate shells that are used. Klim uses his accounting skills to understate inventories, siphon off 'credits,' and…prepare the various Income Tax Returns."

The judge wrote that Klim was routinely paid his $100-per-day rate by county taxpayers while he vacationed in Europe to visit his daughter and grandchild or ran errands for Schonek.

O'Kicki said:

Wid's political and financial influence over the Cambria County Commissioners is such that they would not question Klim's ghost payroll payments. Klim was also paid for days that he traveled to Delaware to deliver cash to Joe Biden's presidential campaign headquarters. (Ask Mary Ann Rager or Peter Macesich who heard Klim brag about it in the Cambria County Courthouse.)

The Cambria County minutes (or salary board minutes) will show that Klim was initially hired on June 2, 1980 at the rate of $30.70 per day (page 261); that his status was changed to professional employee on June 16, 1981 (page 105 of minute book) and paid $100 for each and every eight hour day required in the performance of his services; and that Ron Stephenson, personal friend and politically ally of Wid Schonek, changed rates on or about August 15, 1986 (page 325 of minute book) to a $20,000 per year contract back dated to March 1, 1986. The contract was immediately questioned by [me], with respect to Exhibit A, of that contract, Klim's duties.

Perhaps notably, O'Kicki had taken a much different tone on Klim just a few years earlier. The judge was effusive in his praise for Klim as a watchdog in a 1987 Associated Press interview about the accountant's services with the county orphans court.

"I like to keep the barn door locked before the horse is stolen, before the assets are dissipated," O'Kicki said in 1987. "It's very difficult to find the assets for repayment afterward."

The reporter noted that Cambria County was the only county in Pennsylvania that required guardians to file regular financial accountings. O'Kicki devised the system, he had said, to ensure that guardians of patients in state mental institutions, for instance, were not taking advantage of their wards.

Klim said in the article:

Judge O'Kicki put teeth into the law. There was no system before. He was very seriously concerned whether the money was spent properly on the elderly.

If you knew there was not a thorough examination of expenses, there's an opportunity to do something wrong, to do a little finagling. Now, an attorney or an accountant is going to think twice before he does something because Judge O'Kicki steps on them and steps on them hard.

It's possible that either O'Kicki was playing along with the Klim "ghost payroll payments" or that Klim had in fact been providing a valuable service and had only evoked the fugitive judge's ire for being in Schonek's camp.

Beyond the Klim allegations, O'Kicki asserted that Schonek used his political patronage for illegal favors and racketeering. He said bedsheets from the county-owned Laurel Crest Manor were converted to rags and distributed to his auto supply stores and that stocking supplies from other governmental sources were also diverted to his personal businesses. He accused Green's brother Vernon of arranging for fifty-five-gallon drums of paint to be diverted from the Cambria County airport to one of Schonek's businesses along Eisenhower Boulevard.

City towing services provided by Ed Cernic Sr., O'Kicki claimed, were part of another Schonek pay-to-play scheme.

"Ed Cernic has a present 1988–89 contract for towing illegally parked cars in the City of Johnstown," the judge wrote. "He pays an extra $100 (plus) on each Dick's Automotive invoice. The excess is then paid to the mayor by Wid Schonek. Attorney Dick Green is the solicitor for the City of Johnstown and for Wid Schonek."

O'Kicki further characterized Schonek as a pervasive political influencer with mob connections:

> *Joseph "Little Joe" Regino, well known organized crime figure in Western PA, was a daily visitor to FOUR SEASONS prior to his death. His golf locker in the "Silo Club" remains sealed out of respect to his memory. Nobody else can use that locker even today, August, 1989. "Wid" and "Little Joe" were political partners and were involved in business together. "Little Joe" was the overseer of the numbers, horseracing, sports betting and loan sharking in the Cambria, Somerset and Blair County areas. FOUR SEASONS (believed to also be Relaxation, Inc.) and Penn Sota, Inc. are the places that wealth is siphoned to for the sole benefit of Wid Schonek, Dick Green and Tony Klim.*
>
> *On August 24, 1989, at the FOUR SEASONS resort in Somerset County, PA, a steak, shrimp and booze party was [held]. Attendance was by invitation only. PA State Supreme Court Justice Rolf Larsen was there. So was Senator Joseph Biden from [Delaware], Judges Swope, Long and Leahey of Cambria County Court, District Attorney Creany and his father, Senior Judge Creany, Somerset County District Attorney Flowers, [Johnstown mayor] Herb Pfuhl, Cambria County Commissioners Stephenson and Roberts, Sheriff Jay Roberts and 500 other politicians or political workers. All expenses for this party were paid out of the corporate accounts and charged off in prior years as "business expense."*

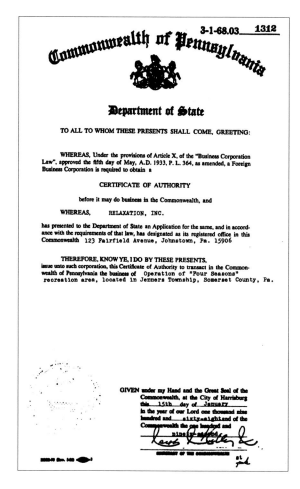

Left: This 1968 certificate from the commonwealth established Relaxation Inc. as a corporate entity permitted to operate the Four Seasons Resort in Jenner Township. Wilbur E. "Wid" Schonek was the owner of the property and Relaxation Inc.'s secretary treasurer. *Courtesy of the Pennsylvania Department of State.*

Opposite: The first page of "The Players," a Joe O'Kicki manifesto alleging illegal activities by Wilbur "Wid" Schonek. This document does not include hard evidence to support these claims. *Courtesy of Sylvia Onusic.*

According to O'Kicki, these political rallies had gone on for at least a decade. Liquor for the events, he said, was brought up from Maryland, in violation of state law. He noted that Pennsylvania State Police had brought no action against Schonek despite tips from informants to liquor enforcement in both Altoona and Somerset.

In 1986 I was invited to my first "Four Seasons Picnic." This was a corn on the cob and steak feast with all the liquor one could consume for elected officials and other guests from the Cambria and Somerset County areas. I later learned from the [RICO] action filed in 1989…federal court that the liquor for these parties was bought by the Hancock Maryland store and the untaxed liquor was brought across state lines by Wid.

I   THE PLAYERS

  A. WILBUR "WID" SCHONEK, 843 Franco Avenue, Johnstown, PA 15905

    1. Father-in-law of Lt. Govenor Mark Singel

    2. Financial Godfather for

      a. Senator Joseph Biden

      b. Senator Arlen Spector

      c. Johnstown Mayor Herb Pfuhl

      d. County Commissioners Ron Stephenson, Joseph Roberts

      e. District Attorney Tim Creany

      f. County Judges Caram Abood and Gerry Long

      g. District Magistrates Farra, Rozum and Yesonosky

  B. Attorney RICHARD J. GREEN, 305 Franklin Street, Johnstown, PA 15901

    1. Johnstown City Solicitor

    2. Former Johnstown School Board Member

    3. Former PA State Senator

    4. Personal Solicitor and daily luncheon companion of Wid Schonek; 20% of his annual fees come from Wid Schonek. (See Court Case, SCHONEK vs NELSON, Florida).

  C. ANTHONY KLIM, 263 Laurel Avenue, Johnstown, PA 15906

    1. Retired IRS Auditor

    2. Controller for Wid Schonek and his companies for the past 25 years. (See court case SCHONEK vs NELSON, Florida).

II PLAYTHINGS

  A. PENNSYLVANIA CORPORATIONS

    1. Dick's Automotive Company (3 stores in Johnstown, 1 in Homer City and St. Michael).

    2. Cove Auto Supply, Inc.

    3. Roof Garden Auto Supply

    4. Turnpike Auto Supply   7. Greencastle Auto Supply

    5. McConnellsburg Auto Supply, Inc. 8. Jenners Auto Supply

    6. Penn-Sota, Inc.   9. Academy Auto Supply-Mercersburg

  B. FLORIDA CORPORATIONS

    1. Sunshine State Supply, Inc.

    2. Gulf Coast Auto Supply, Inc.

    3. Par-Tele, Inc.

    4. Gateport, Inc.

O'Kicki stated that Schonek never filed federal or state returns for the resort and that Pennsylvania sales tax had gone unfiled and uncollected. He alleged that expenses and wages were paid by Jenners Auto Supply.

"Steel for the swimming pool and the main building of FOUR SEASONS 'came from' the Johnstown Plant of Bethlehem Steel (as did plumbing, wiring, etc.). Check the annual stockholder minutes of Bethlehem in 1980–1982 for details," the judge wrote.

Many of the accusations leveled by O'Kicki echoed claims of criminal fraud, tax evasion and bribery outlined by Rudolph "Boots" Schonek in a 1989 civil suit against his brother. Each Schonek accused the other of racketeering.

In a memo to the Supreme Court of Pennsylvania's eastern district, O'Kicki also called for the immediate suspension and disbarment of Green, the attorney who testified that O'Kicki had demanded a kickback from him after awarding a settlement to a client. The former judge wrote:

> *Richard J. Green has been for the past 35 years or more and still is the personal attorney of Wilbur "Wid" Schonek, a political power broker in Pennsylvania and owner of a chain of 26 auto parts stores in Pennsylvania, Maryland, Florida, and other states. Exhibit A, a caption [from] a Rico lawsuit filed in Federal Court, lists the various names of the various entities and is attached hereto and made a part hereof.*

O'Kicki accused Green of violating the code of professional responsibility by telling Wid Schonek about the contents of his brother's will when Boots decided to give money to a local church charitable institution. Wid asked O'Kicki to talk to Boots about changing this and giving the money instead to the "Wid Schonek Pension Fund."

Regarding the unpaid loans he'd been accused of taking from Green, O'Kicki characterized them as repayment. O'Kicki argued that he had sold his law practice to Green and Caram Abood when he was elected judge. A bill of sale dated December 27, 1971, states that O'Kicki was offloading his covered furniture, furnishings, books, corporation files, 358 active files and 375 abstract of title files to the duo. The document is signed by all three parties but does not include a notary signature.

O'Kicki accused his former secretary Brenda Nasser—one of the commonwealth's witnesses against him at trial—of hiding or destroying the contract at Green's request. O'Kicki noted that Green represented Nasser when O'Kicki fired her in 1980. He cited testimony from his criminal trial that indicated Nasser had also been romantically involved with Schonek.

While suing Green and Abood over his law practice, O'Kicki demanded that Cambria County judge Norman A. Krumenacker III recuse himself. O'Kicki claimed that Krumenacker had a conflict of interest because he had once served as his law clerk. He also characterized Krumenacker as an "active political and financial supporter" of Abood with ties to Green, a former law partner of Krumenacker's father.

***

DURING A PHONE INTERVIEW in January 2021, Fran Mattre recalled her time working for Wid. She said her boyfriend's sister was the businessman's secretary. Mattre herself started working for him under the table at Dick's Automotive when she was fifteen and was put on the official payroll when she was sixteen, clocking her hours primarily after school and on weekends.

Mattre said that she handled invoicing, receipts, bookkeeping and cash register duties, and she remembered that Schonek had a close relationship with Bethlehem Steel executives, including Ted Helsel.

"Ted [Helsel] and Wid were so, so tight," Mattre said, noting that she saw between twenty-five and thirty Bethlehem Steel invoices on some days. "I wonder how many things were purchased in the name of Bethlehem Steel?

"Without even knowing it, we were part of his cover."

Like O'Kicki, Mattre sensed connections between Schonek and the mob. She and the other office girls were often treated to free meals at the Mafia-owned Shangri-La club. It was there that a teenage Mattre said she had her first drink—a daquiri, if memory served.

"They didn't seem like the typical Johnstown businessmen [at Shangri-La]," she said.

"It was kind of set back in the woods. They always had someone there to take your car. It was kind of like a romantic, dark, very low-lit, very pretty kind of intimate place. You felt that it was very private."

Also like O'Kicki, Mattre recalled Schonek hosting after-hours gatherings with important clients in the upper apartment quarters at 123 Fairfield Avenue in Johnstown.

"His associates—whatever associates they were—they would stay there. These were people of influence," she said.

"There were just people who came in and out. I knew there were shady things going on because of how he kept the books and had these separate apartments. You just knew there were things that were going on that weren't right."

In all, Mattre said she worked for Schonek part time for three summers and full time for an additional year.

This building at 123–27 Fairfield Avenue in Johnstown—now occupied by Bent Wookee Comix, a graphic novel store—was once home to a business entity known as Penn-Sota Inc. Millionaire Cambria County businessman Wilbur "Wid" Schonek supposedly hosted parties on the third floor of this building for Bethlehem Steel executives and other influential people. *Courtesy of Shayna Nardecchia.*

"He was a gentleman," she said. "He was gruff but a sweetheart."

When Schonek died in 2001 at the age of eighty-eight, public speculation regarding his will was immediate. The *Tribune-Democrat* noted that his "political cronies"—namely Biden, former Johnstown police chief Robert Huntley, former mayor Herb Pfuhl and City Councilman Anthony "Red" Pinizzotto—did not receive a cut.

Pinizzotto, seemingly miffed by the snub, told the newspaper, "I've got my thoughts, but I'm not going to share them. It's [Schonek's] prerogative, I guess."

Attempts to reach President Biden about his relationship with Schonek were unsuccessful. But record exists of him accepting money from the Johnstown powerbroker. A June 1, 1990 article in the *Daily Times* noted that Biden had repaid a $10,000 personal loan to Schonek. And it was reported that he attended Schonek's funeral in 2001.

"Wid had a very good way of sizing up people," Mattre said. "He could size them up pretty quick."

Chapter 13

LAWYERS, DRUGS AND MURDER

I n the portrait of reality painted by Joe O'Kicki, society was hopelessly infused with corruption. There was systemic voter fraud and abuse of power, from the capitol in Harrisburg to the streets of small towns across the commonwealth. He claimed to have inside knowledge of narcotics trafficking, political assassinations and the backstory to the most infamous example of public suicide in recent memory.

In his letter to U.S. attorney general Janet Reno, the judge said that drug dealing flourished in Cambria County under a "tacit understanding" with the Pennsylvania attorney general, state police and local courts. He claimed that a "crack house" in Flinton had remained in operation since 1991 despite constant complaints to state police, the district attorney and a drug task force. He stated that drug penalties were being softened against a few select locals because of family ties and community connections. O'Kicki added that he believed Nicholas Kush—one of the Outlaw bikers he'd sentenced in the state police shooting and fight at the Snack Shack tavern in 1980—had been given oral work release as early as 1989 even though he shouldn't have been eligible for this until 2001 based on minimum sentencing guidelines.

The judge also made ominous reference to drug smuggling at the airport in Richland Township. "A DC-3 loaded with cocaine and marijuana flew non-stop from Columbia [sic] and landed in Johnstown. The pilot and co-pilot were never found. Nor was the cocaine," O'Kicki wrote. "How did the pilot know that the Johnstown airport was closed from midnight Sunday to 6 a.m. Monday? The plane was returned to owner because 'the commonwealth failed to prove that the owner had knowledge of the illegal use of his plane.'"

O'Kicki asserted that freight corruption was commonplace by land as well.

> *Robert Colondo of the…state police informed students at the University of Pittsburgh, Johnstown in February 1988 and 1989, while guest lecturing at a criminal justice course, that arrests for overweight trucks were no longer being made because of the inability to secure convictions in Cambria County court. All cases are heard by the same judge, who regularly dismisses the complaints. These violations occur on U.S. Routes 219 and 22.*
>
> *One law firm, with close association with organized crime, handles or distributes the defenses of such arrests when made. Trucking companies are called by that law firm for "political contributions" for political campaigns such as Preate's in 1988.*

He further extended his charges to the banking industry. The judge wrote that Michael Gulino, a man "listed as the boss of organized crime in Cambria County by the Pa Crime Commission (See Pennsylvania Crime Commission Report, 1990)," was given a $100,000 line of credit by a local bank in spite of his well-known mob ties.

O'Kicki even opined on homicides.

> *Dan Galiczynski, a 23 year old white male from Barnesboro, Pennsylvania shot and killed one black person and wounded another on the streets of Johnstown. He entered a plea bargain for Third Degree Murder and was sentenced to serve 10 to 20 years. However, he served less than one year in confinement, including time spent for mental evaluations. "Someone forgot" for 8 years to bring him back to jail after being sent to a Teen Challenge Program. No work release order was ever issued.*
>
> *He had been working at a car wash in Lancaster, and returned to Cambria County Jail.*

The colloquially famous cold case of Mafia numbers writer Joseph "Pippy" DiFalco was also addressed. O'Kicki noted that DiFalco—whose lifeless body was found stabbed and dumped in the Conemaugh Dam Reservoir in 1960—was among forty unsolved murders in a county of fewer than 180,000 residents. He inferred that DiFalco's homicide and the more recent death of a local judge were connected to organized crime.

In July 1983, a Muenster Township farmer found the car of Judge Joseph McCabe, a magistrate from the Cambria County community of Portage, parked inexplicably on his property. Portage police searched the farmer's land and soon found McCabe's body in a wooded area approximately one hundred yards from the vehicle. A wire report published in the *Pittsburgh Post-Gazette* said a state police spokesman confirmed that "at least one gunshot wound" was found in McCabe's body.

O'Kicki called McCabe's death "an alleged suicide" and implied that it was "related to continuing crime activities" in the area. His doubt about the official story was something already expressed by fellow judge and political enemy Gerald Long, who questioned the situation as district attorney years prior.

As wild as these claims were, they were easily outdone by an O'Kicki allegation related to the political bombshell best known as the CTA scandal.

IN 1986, PENNSYLVANIA STATE treasurer R. Budd Dwyer and former Pennsylvania GOP chairman Robert Asher were indicted on charges of participating in a bribery scheme. They were accused of helping a company called Computer Technology Associates, aka CTA, secure a no-bid multimillion-dollar contract in exchange for a $300,000 campaign contribution.

CTA had been hired to recover approximately $40 million in overpayments of Social Security taxes by school districts and their employees. The company was owned by Johnstown native John Torquato Jr. of the Torquato Democratic political dynasty.

Torquato Jr.'s father, John Torquato Sr., was the longtime chairman of the Cambria County Democratic Party and a member of the National Democratic Committee who earned the nickname of "Scare" and "Big John" for his prominence on the political scene. In 1978, he was charged with—and later convicted of—extortion and conspiracy. He was found to be "squeezing" Pennsylvania Department of Transportation contractors for kickbacks and served twenty months in jail. Torquato Sr. was acquitted of mail fraud charges for having a county Democratic headquarters employee on state and county payrolls.

Like his father, Torquato Jr. ended up serving time. He pleaded guilty to conspiracy and was sentenced to four years in prison. Attorneys in courtroom testimony vehemently argued that he was the mastermind of the CTA scandal, a "con man and alcoholic" who used a "magic show" to seduce his co-conspirators.

"There are not too many people like John Torquato in the world," lawyer Caton Machamer said during the trial. "He is a brilliant man...but he is also insidious.

"I give you the test—would you take John Torquato home and introduce him to your daughter?"

In his 1993 letter to Reno, O'Kicki claimed to have insight on the CTA case. He implied that a miscarriage of justice was involved.

"The [Pennsylvania] Attorney General and State Police use the criminal justice system for political gain," he said. "Banks can call upon them to use the criminal process to collect civil debts....In Dauphin County, the wife of Attorney William Smith was threatened with arrest in the CTA case until her husband pled guilty and became the star witness against State Treasurer Budd Dwyer."

In the wake of his conviction, Dwyer became a tragic case study in media ethics when he infamously shot and killed himself during a televised press conference. Debate about whether TV and press should have run the video or photos of this chilling public suicide continues in journalism classrooms to this day.

Further referencing this well-known saga, O'Kicki told Reno that the "murder in Harrisburg in 1988 of State Representative William Telek is directly related to the CTA case and organized crime. Telek was able to place Pa Attorney General [LeRoy] Zimmerman in the CTA case with John Torquato Jr."

This, perhaps on multiple levels, was an incredible statement. The fugitive judge was telling the chief law enforcement official in America that a Pennsylvania legislator was the victim of a hit because of his knowledge on a political scandal that led to several high-profile corruption convictions and the most well-known public suicide of the twentieth century.

At minimum, it's true that Zimmerman was under scrutiny at the height of the CTA scandal. His former press secretary at the Pennsylvania Office of Attorney General told prosecutors that Torquato and Smith offered his boss a $100,000 campaign contribution in exchange for a favorable legal opinion on CTA. Torquato testified in support of this claim, but Smith and Zimmerman refuted it, and the attorney general was never convicted in relation to the scandal. Zimmerman did not respond to a recent email asking for comment on CTA and O'Kicki's allegations.

AT APPROXIMATELY 1:30 A.M. on May 17, 1988—a few years after Dwyer's death and other CTA fallout—Telek was dropped off at the capitol's annex parking garage by fellow state representative Edgar Carlson. His body was discovered an hour or so later in the middle of Bergner Street, a wooded and "isolated, poorly lit" area just outside the Harrisburg city limits. Telek's pants had been pulled down and his left pants pocket pulled inside out. His death was caused by three heavy hits from a blunt object.

A few hours later, police spotted Telek's 1987 Chrysler Fifth Avenue sedan near the Harrisburg High School campus. A high-speed chase followed over the span of several miles before ending in the shadow of the capitol building. The driver, a seventeen-year-old Black teen named Bernard Williams, was accompanied by John and Brian Anderson, also minors.

According to court records, Williams provided police with conflicting accounts. He told an officer he bought the vehicle for $100 from someone named "Tom Smith" near Friendly's Bar along Third Street less than an hour before he was pulled over. Then he said he'd purchased the sedan and a dime of "herb" from someone named "Tim Smith" the night before. Police testified that Williams made a series of unsolicited statements such as, "They dumped the body in Susquehanna Township," and, "The old man must have been uptown to buy drugs," before officers had even mentioned a murder. A search warrant was executed at the teen's home, and a ball hammer was found in the headboard of his bed. It contained traces of human blood.

Though the amount of human blood was not substantial enough for further testing, a pathologist testified that he was able to say with a reasonable degree of medical certainty that the wounds to Telek's face and skull were caused by a hammer exactly like the one owned by Williams. He was convicted of first-degree murder and sentenced to life without the possibility of parole. His Post Conviction Relief Act appeals, including one in 2019, have been summarily rejected. The record reflects that Williams participated in thirty-six prison assaults between 1997 and 2017. He also shanked a corrections officer in 1993.

If O'Kicki had corroborating evidence that Telek's murder was an organized crime hit rather than an act of random street violence resulting from a carjacking and theft, it was absent from the cache of documents provided by his wife. This claim, and most others in the Reno letter, are explosive but lacking in proof—an indication that perhaps the judge was reaching in an effort to gain audience with the attorney general and barter for his pension or freedom.

Nevertheless, O'Kicki provided an extensive interview to Harrisburg author William Keisling in which he made sensational claims about Zimmerman and corrupt party politics across the commonwealth. He told Keisling how he was expected to give 2 percent of his salary back to the Cambria County Democratic Committee after being hired as the assistant county solicitor and donated closer to 5 percent. He claimed that candidates can directly purchase votes through union bosses and political chairs who fill out their constituents' ballots for them all across Pennsylvania. And he recounted a story in which he unwittingly served as courier for $10,000 from Johnstown cocaine trafficker Frank Romani to the attorney general in 1983.

O'Kicki doubled-down on the Romani-Zimmerman claim in a subsequent television interview. He said:

> *I also worked with Cambria County businessman Frank Romani, who had no history of any heart problem whatsoever and three weeks after the book* Maybe Four Steps *is printed, in which he's named in there as having given money to the former attorney general LeRoy Zimmerman...Frank Romani is found dead in his cell of a heart attack.*
>
> *That isn't coincidence. That, in my humble judgment, is indication of how the system can silence those who want to expose the corruption.*

O'Kicki characterized himself as one of those people being silenced for their efforts in exposing corruption. He settled on another theory that the root of his legal problems stemmed from his willingness to take on injustices of the 1977 Johnstown Flood.

Chapter 14

THE FLOOD

Tony Piskurich has never forgotten July 19, 1977.

On this date, Piskurich and his wife—though they were only dating at the time—spent the evening at St. Rochus Church at the corner of Chestnut and Eighth Streets in Johnstown's Cambria City neighborhood. They were rehearsing for a festival as part of the church folk group when the downpour began. Sometime after 9:00 p.m., the office manager informed them that Broad Street was flooded. Members of the group were offered the opportunity to spend the night at church facilities to avoid the dangerous drive. Piskurich talked to his mother over the phone, who urged him to do just that.

"She goes, 'Son, don't come home because the dip [is] flooded,'" Piskurich recalled during an interview forty-five years later. "The dip was a low spot on Cooper Avenue where we lived."

The priest of the parish tried to drive him home after midnight, but they found the intersection of Prosser Hollow Road and Iron Street impassable, blocked by rushing water, branches and entire trees. So he and some others slept in the church's convent.

Before daybreak, the twenty-four-year-old Piskurich was wakened from a couch on the convent basement. Things, he was told, had gone from bad to worse.

They attempted to drive to higher ground, but the van was flooded out. Abandoning the vehicle, they walked up and over the bridge toward Brownstown. They were astonished by the scene.

Tony Piskurich during a 2019 interview at the Venue of Merging Arts, aka VOMA, in Johnstown's Cambria City neighborhood. He was among those who lost loved ones in the 1977 Johnstown Flood. *Photo by Eric Kieta/*Daily American.

"We saw railroad tank cars come floating down the river…toward the Coopersdale bridge," Piskurich said. "We could see all of this going on, and it was horrifying."

Piskurich eventually made it to his aunt's house. He was told soon thereafter that the Laurel Run Dam may have collapsed.

"That was my first inkling that we had a problem. I said to myself, 'If that thing went, and went with any force, it's going to be bad,'" he said.

Piskurich waded his way back down to Cambria City, to St. Rochus, where he found that the raging waters had turned his car completely around. He trudged on, down Broad Street, to the Coopersdale bridge, and saw the cars piled brokenly against telephone poles. At the head of a path, the shortcut to his home, he saw a man.

"He looked at me and he said, 'Tony, you don't want to go out there. There's nothing left,'" Piskurich said.

At one of the rescue centers in neighboring Westwood, Piskurich found his uncle's name listed as a survivor.

"He looked like he had been through the ringer in a prizefight," Piskurich said. "[I said] 'Unc, what about Mom and Dad?'"

Piskurich's uncle and parents had been in their home when floodwaters literally broke the residence apart. His uncle recounted how he heard Piskurich's father yell his mother's name and then no more from them as they were swept downstream. He eventually managed to grasp onto a building and rode out the rest of the '77 Flood on the roof of a steel mill.

"It was pretty harrowing. I'm just amazed he survived," Piskurich said. "A strong man, good swimmer and lucky."

His parents, however, were not lucky. Piskurich later identified his mother by her wedding ring and his father by his wallet. He was barred from seeing either one of them.

Their home had been leveled. Five blocks of the concrete garage was all that remained.

Because of the circumstances, the call Piskurich made to his mom from the church the night of the flood has been unforgettable.

"I was never thinking it'd be the last time I'd hear her voice," he said, "but it's strange the way things happen."

AFTER THE GRIEVING AND cleanup from the flood, the victims' families began to ask questions. How did this happen? Were these deaths preventable? And who was responsible?

Nearly half of the eighty-six deaths from the '77 Flood occurred in the Tanneryville community of West Taylor Township. Research compiled by St. Francis University professor Pat Farabaugh indicated that thirty-four residents of this neighborhood were killed. The devastation in Tanneryville is attributable almost entirely to the collapse of Laurel Run Dam, which sat uphill from these homes.

According to Farabaugh, the original dam there was built in 1869 to help the City of Johnstown meet its water needs. It was abandoned in 1910, only to be rebuilt as a "temporary structure" in 1919 by the Cambria Steel Co. affiliate Johnstown Water Co. The dam was 42 feet high, 620 feet long and held up to 101 million gallons of water. Its spillway was capable of passing runoff water at a rate of 2,100 cubic feet per second. The problem, according to multiple engineers over a span of several decades, was that this spillway was less than half the size it should have been.

In the mid-1990s, records unsealed by a Cambria County judge revealed that studies indicated safety concerns with the dam decades before its collapse. A Philadelphia engineer named Charles Haydock in 1943 told management at Bethlehem Steel, which owned the dam, that Laurel Run was among four area dams that had fallen short of current standards. Because Bethlehem was in negotiations at the time with Johnstown officials who were interested in buying Laurel Run, Haydock recommended setting $200,000 aside to make spillway improvements.

But Bethlehem rebuffed the idea. A vice president for the corporation penned an inter-office memo that said, in part, "Had there been difficulties at any time, the necessary changes would have been made."

Haydock's findings were reaffirmed in 1959 by D'Appolonia, a Pittsburgh engineering firm. D'Appolonia's study noted that the spillway's runoff capability rate should have been increased to 6,200 cubic feet per second, which was essentially a tripling of its existing capacity. Engineers also pointed out that soil samples removed from the dam's center indicated structural weaknesses.

Deficiencies be damned, the newly founded Greater Johnstown Water Authority purchased the dam from Bethlehem in 1963. Day-to-day management was outsourced to Laurel Management, an outgrowth of Johnstown Water Co., and Gannett Fleming Corddry & Carpenter was retained as consulting engineers. Attorneys would argue behind closed doors after the 1977 disaster that the water company wasn't privy to these safety concerns, despite a 1970 state report classifying Laurel Run as a "high-hazard" dam with the potential of "causing both life and property losses."

Piskurich was among those who filed civil suits against these entities after losing his loved ones. He and the others watched and waited as these cases

The 1977 Johnstown flood destroyed this house along Messenger Street in the Hornerstown neighborhood. *Courtesy of Jerry McDevitt.*

Passersby look on at a car partially submerged in mud and sediment at the intersection of Johnstown's Central Avenue and Ohio Street in the wake of the 1977 flood. *Courtesy of Jerry McDevitt.*

languished in a purgatorial status at the Cambria County Courthouse deep into the 1980s.

"For some reason, the suit didn't go anywhere," Piskurich said. "[We suspected] there was an interference...major players who all seemed to know each other. Things did kind of grind to a halt."

A growing chorus of discontent arose. In September 1984, the *Tribune-Review* interviewed several attorneys over a six-day span. The lawyers—their identities shielded for fear of retribution for publicly criticizing the local judiciary—were "bluntly critical" of Cambria County president judge H. Clifton McWilliams, suggesting that a seventeen-month delay between class-action certification hearings was unnecessarily long.

"These cases could have been in posture for trial two years ago," one said.

McWilliams disagreed. He noted the complexity of handling a situation that involved more than one hundred plaintiffs and multiple defendants, both private and governmental.

"We have so many attorneys and so many parties involved in this thing, it is like pulling teeth to get things done, there's no doubt about it.... The only thing I can tell you is I didn't take a vacation this year," McWilliams said. "You show me any attorneys who didn't get one and I'll be very surprised. We're going to move this and we're going to resolve it."

But it wasn't moved and it wasn't resolved, at least not during McWilliams's tenure. All sides punted responsibility. Water authority attorney Samuel DiFrancesco said, "Bethlehem sold the water authority a pig in a poke; that was a theory that was being put forth, that if there was anything wrong with the Laurel Run dam it preexisted the purchase and was not revealed to us."

Charles Kunkle, top shareholder of Laurel Management and former general manager of the dam, said: "We never had any trouble with the spillway other than the concrete deteriorating. We never had any problems with it raining eight hours before."

James Romano, former Gannett Fleming president, said: "The engineer couldn't very well come forward and say 'enlarge the spillway' when the Commonwealth of Pennsylvania, who is sovereign in these matters, was not saying so. Gannett Fleming would be put in an untenable position."

A young boy looks on amid scattered bricks, peeling asphalt and debris as lingering water from the 1977 Flood runs down Ohio Street in Johnstown. *Courtesy of Jerry McDevitt.*

According to Piskurich, the only person of any community stature who seemed to be making any sense about the 1977 Flood was the man who soon became a community pariah: Joe O'Kicki. He recalled taking the judge's government and law class at the University of Pittsburgh at Johnstown. Piskurich had recognized him from the newspapers and approached him after lessons one day to tell him about what happened to his parents and ask about the flood cases.

"He looked at me and said, 'It's a terrible shame what's going on with that lawsuit.' He knew about it, and he thought justice was definitely being delayed," Piskurich said.

"He said to me, 'If I become president judge I'll make sure we move these cases along.' He basically got the parties all together and said, 'We've got to get this settled to everybody's satisfaction.'"

True to his word on the matter, it was O'Kicki who kickstarted movement on the civil suits. He'd presided over previous matters of the flood, including a 1979 hearing to declare a missing ten-year-old girl and her forty-one-year-old mother dead after two years missing. The pair had been visiting a trailer along Cooper Avenue when the Laurel Run Dam broke.

As McWilliams approached the state-mandated retirement age of seventy, O'Kicki contacted the Supreme Court of Pennsylvania for an evaluation of backlogs plaguing the civil and criminal dockets. This was the damning report handed to O'Kicki in the summer of 1988 when he was sworn in as president judge.

O'Kicki wrote after his conviction:

> *The Johnstown Flood cases were filed on April 7, 1978. The lawyers delayed these cases in the court system for nearly 11 years. Within two months after becoming President Judge in June of 1988, all of the cases involving more* [than $87] *million dollars in claims were set for the trial. Another judge continued the cases and two years later they were settled. Why no trial in Dec. 1988?*
>
> *Therefore, the report which revealed such flagrant misuse of the county court system, lies abandoned in the back of a dusty drawer or filing cabinet and the behavior, which was described as "shocking and alarming," continues to flourish unabated.*

A *Tribune-Democrat* brief in October 1988 noted that newly promoted President Judge Caram Abood had postponed the flood cases yet again. He cited scheduling conflicts and the fact that O'Kicki, who was then suspended,

Judge Caram Abood looking on as President Judge Joe O'Kicki talks about an "alarming" evaluation of the Cambria County court system during his swearing-in ceremony as president judge on June 3, 1988. *Courtesy of the* Altoona Mirror.

was to preside over this trial. Abood said he had met with lawyers for the defendants and urged them to settle the cases out of court.

This is what ultimately occurred. University of Pittsburgh at Johnstown professor Andrew T. Rose noted in a 2008 study that civil suits from the flood were eventually settled after twelve years of "legal haggling" and that the out-of-court settlements were "considered paltry leaving the victims' families feeling slighted by the sluggish and unsympathetic legal system." He added that the Laurel Run collapse was one of three significant dam failures that directly resulted in the evolution of dam safety laws to include more stringent inspection and enforcement regulations.

"My brother and I didn't get a huge settlement by any stretch of the imagination," Piskurich said.

Payouts ranged from $8,200 to $320,000. The average settlement was $95,000. Legal experts cited by a *Tribune-Democrat* reporter in 1997 characterized these payouts as "skimpy" for wrongful death claims.

"Did [Bethlehem and the water authority] get off easy? Yeah, I think so," Piskurich said. "If they had settled early on, it might have been different.

"Joe O'Kicki knew the reason [for trial delays]. He knew who was involved. I don't think it was fair."

DR. BILL CHOBY, AN area dentist, was another student of O'Kicki's at the Unversity of Pittsburgh at Johnstown. He met with the judge years later to ask for advice when he decided to run for Congress in 1989.

"It's through him that I learned about the flood and that he wanted to clean up those cases," Choby said.

"He relayed to me that he felt that was why [his enemies] were after him. That cabal killed Johnstown."

Choby cited defendants' inadequate insurance as one factor. Court records indicated that Laurel Management was covered for $500,000 and water authority engineers Gannett Fleming for $1 million. The water authority listed its coverage at $250,000. Amherst Insurance, a solicitor for the authority, was to cover the entity for settlements in excess of this insurance but had been insolvent for years. Fellow defendants Bethlehem Steel and the Commonwealth of Pennsylvania were reportedly self-insured.

"They didn't have the money to [cover] it," Choby said regarding the tens of millions in claims. "It was just a fraction of what it should have been."

Farabaugh—who wrote extensively on this subject in his 2021 book, *Disastrous Floods and the Demise of Steel in Johnstown*—noted that Cambria County leaders went to great lengths to keep steel production viable in the region. He said the Johnstown Area Regional Industries organization was formed as a result of this effort.

"This group included many prominent Johnstown businessmen, including Louis Galliker, Daniel Glosser, Frank Pasquerilla, Walter Krebs, Robert Gleason, Andrew Koban, [Laurel Run dam manager] Charles Kunkle, Howard Picking and others. JARI's primary goals were to preserve steel production in the city and identify other areas for economic growth in Cambria County," he said.

"The group did have some success. In 1974—the year JARI was [founded]—it raised $3 million for industrial development in the city."

According to Farabaugh, these economic challenges became increasingly difficult after the devastation of the '77 Flood. He said:

> *Lewis Foy, CEO of Bethlehem Steel at the time of the 1977 flood, probably felt as much pressure as anybody. He grew up on a farm in nearby Shanksville and rose through the ranks at Bethlehem, becoming CEO in 1974. He definitely wanted to keep the steel industry alive in the area.*

After the 1977 Flood, Foy told government officials that he estimated it would cost Bethlehem $35 million to clean up and rebuild equipment and facilities that were damaged. Charles Kunkle, president of the Johnstown Water Authority, flew to the Lehigh Valley and met with Foy shortly after the flood. Kunkle tried to convince Foy to invest in getting Bethlehem's operations in Johnstown back up and running. Foy ultimately did approve funds for clean-up and rebuilding efforts, but he told Kunkle that plans to resume work on a basic oxygen furnace in Johnstown—one that was roughly half completed at the time of the flood—were not moving forward.

By the end of 1977, Farabaugh said, approximately 7,300 Bethlehem employees in Johnstown had lost their jobs. Could this have created a climate in which, as O'Kicki implied, the cases were delayed deliberately?

"It's conceivable. Government and business leaders obviously want to keep people employed in good-paying jobs in their regions. This is true in Johnstown, just as it is everywhere else," Farabaugh said.

"Did Johnstown leaders want to keep Bethlehem officials interested in continuing steel making in the city and not do anything to jeopardize this

At left is one of Johnstown's historic steel mills. The city has yet to recover economically from the departure of mega employer Bethlehem Steel. *Courtesy of Layne Siwy.*

interest? Yes. Now, whether or not this created a hesitancy to push forward legal action against Bethlehem following the flood, I don't know."

As for whether the Tanneryville deaths could have been prevented with sufficient investment from Bethlehem or subsequent water authority management, a haunting assessment from an engineer who reviewed the dam years before it broke left no uncertainty.

"Laurel Run is well known to me," Elio D'Appolonia wrote in 1977. "We investigated this dam in the '60s. Its deficiencies were recognized and reports prepared for modification, but for various reasons, over a period of one and a half decades, remedial steps or new construction was not undertaken.

"If the dam had been upgraded in accordance with today's—prudent—engineering practice, the dam would have been able to store and/or pass the storm."

Chapter 15

CLOSING ARGUMENTS

I n some of the last known footage of the former judge, he wanders an orange desert-like Mediterranean landscape. He drifts across the screen, a balding reprobate Moses of sorts, exiled in a white polo and black dress pants.

He told a WWCP reporter that "The Fix," his tell-all memoir, was nearly complete.

"The system needs [to be] slapped in the face. The system is corrupt," O'Kicki said.

"I have a first draft written. It deals with the legal system of Pennsylvania. And in about two months it should be completed....We'll see what we do after that."

His writing, however, took a backseat to more pressing matters.

"He was gathering information and he wrote a lot of letters," Sylvia Onusic said. "He wrote so many things to his attorneys if I just gathered that into a book and edited it that would be 'The Fix.'"

The judge's health took a turn for the worse. In September 1995, he had a second cancer operation.

"He had...colorectal cancer, two main sites," Onusic said. "And they took out the cancer, they gave him chemo, they gave him radiation, all that. And he endured all that and other therapies. But when he was in Slovenia the cancer came back....He had it removed, but then after that it was all downhill. I mean, he was just too weak."

By the early weeks of 1997, the news was out. Dr. Dusan Keber, who had worked on a graduate degree with Onusic in Slovenia, provided no

A recent photograph of Ljubljana, Slovenia. *Courtesy of Tim Burns.*

details, but the gist was this: O'Kicki had died.

Back in America, reactions were varied. Cynics and skeptics wanted proof. Didn't the fugitive jurist have an interest in authorities simply believing he was gone?

"Our position is that we need to verify that he is dead," Sean Duffy, a spokesman for Pennsylvania attorney general Mike Fisher, said once news of O'Kicki's passing reached home more than two months later.

Cambria County judge Gerald Long echoed this sentiment: "I just wonder if he's really dead."

To this day, Onusic said, she's pained by these accusations. She believes this sort of talk—that her husband would fake his death—is meant to hurt her. She said:

> He was actually functioning until the very end when he couldn't drink or eat anymore and he was in such pain....I called the ambulance and they took him there just so he could get some pain medication. But he died shortly thereafter.
>
> They called me from the cancer hospital. Because I worked for the ministry of health, so they knew me. And they said your husband passed away, so I went over there right away, and I saw him.

According to Onusic, O'Kicki died on December 2, 1996, and was buried four days later in Ljubljana's Zale Cemetery, directly across the street from where his parents had married many decades earlier. He was sixty-six years old.

His tell-all memoir was another source of speculation. Some in the Johnstown area have claimed to catch glimpses of this little black book. Onusic said state police have even questioned her about it.

"I really never found a finished manuscript," Onusic said. "I found bits and pieces of it."

A look at the gravesite of Joseph O'Kicki in Slovenia. *Courtesy of Sylvia Onusic.*

Those who liked or respected O'Kicki grieved the fact that he ran out of time to redeem himself in the public eye. Attorney Arthur Cohan said the judge had once outlined Pennsylvania's widespread corruption to him.

"It's unfortunate that the matters that caused his leaving to Slovenia were not resolved so that he could come back here with a clean slate," Cohen said.

Lawyer Richard Galloway, who represented O'Kicki at trial, shared similar notions.

"In some ways, I still feel Joseph O'Kicki was the object of a vendetta or something close to that. I'm aware of what the jury said, but I think if he had a trial in a more neutral forum, there might have been a different result," Galloway said.

In another twist, the ink of O'Kicki's obituary had barely dried when new allegations surfaced. A petition from Dennis Anderson of the Outlaws gang was heard before Cambria County judge Norman A. Krumenacker III in 1998.

Anderson—one of the seven bikers convicted of assaulting three police officers at the Snack Shack tavern in 1980—said that O'Kicki had sought a bribe from him and the other gang members. He claimed that O'Kicki promised them a more lenient jail term if they paid him $25,000 each and wanted them to arrange for the contract killing of his first wife or give him a .22-caliber gun with a silencer.

Subsequent hearings kept the ex-judge's name in the spotlight, at least in Cambria County. Anderson testified that he was first brought to the office of then–jail warden Roy Gittings in the summer of 1983. There, he said, he found O'Kicki behind Gittings's desk. He told Krumenacker that the judge offered to "help" him at sentencing, writing "$25,000 each" and ".22 rifle with silencer" on a notepad. Anderson said O'Kicki also wrote something about contacting Outlaw "Taco," president of the group's national chapter, before dismissing him.

According to Anderson, Gittings walked him down the street to O'Kicki's office for a noon meeting just a few hours later. There, he said, O'Kicki

The former jailhouse in Ebensburg has been abandoned in recent years. This is the site of an alleged meeting between Judge Joseph O'Kicki and Dennis Anderson of the Outlaws gang. The biker told authorities O'Kicki offered him a reduced sentence in exchange for $25,000, a .22-caliber pistol with a silencer and a contract for the gang to kill his first wife, Theresa. *Photo by Bruce Siwy.*

repeated his request to meet with "Taco" in Hershey, stating that he'd be there in August for a judges' conference and wanted to "discuss taking care of his old lady."

"Again, where do you go from brilliant to crazy? I mean, the janitors are here.…There are people that come in and out of here at all hours," Krumenacker said in a recent interview about Anderson-O'Kicki meetings. "How are you going to keep a secret like that?"

"His behavior [in the 1980s] was getting so strange. And this is a little courthouse.…You can't keep any secrets here."

R. Bruce Dillon, another ex-Outlaw, was also called to testify in 1998. He told Krumenacker he met O'Kicki alone at an Ebensburg diner in 1982 or 1983. The judge, Dillon said, talked about handling a problem with "some guy in Harrisburg." There was no mention of his wife.

Though the warden confirmed that he helped O'Kicki arrange the private chats with Anderson, former Cambria County prosecutor Dennis McGlynn noted that "police were unable to corroborate the allegations because no one was present at the meetings but O'Kicki and Anderson." Krumenacker said he didn't doubt Anderson's story but ruled against the biker because the evidence indicated that the apparent bribe took place after his sentencing, not before.

———

AT CAMBRIA COUNTY'S STORIED courthouse in Ebensburg, judges of old are immortalized with wall-hung portraits. Its most well-known jurist, however, remains a notable absence. At some point it vanished. No one, not even O'Kicki's widow, knows where it ended up. She discussed at one point offering a reward for it.

The missing portrait, like many aspects of the O'Kicki legacy, is steeped in scandal, mystery and no small element of controversy.

"Everybody kinda knew and were afraid that the judge was gonna become in charge. Because they knew as president judge he could…get things working," said Brian Sukenik, the former courthouse employee who helped O'Kicki investigate questionable practices in the domestic relations office. "And that was the last thing they wanted to do was to spoil the little side arrangements they all had. And I mean 'they' as in attorneys and officers of the court and other members of the commissioners' staff."

Gone like the O'Kicki portrait is the 1988 analysis from the Administrative Office of Pennsylvania Courts—the one that Justice John Flaherty said painted Cambria County in an "alarming" light. Krumenacker's executive assistant said that the Cambria County court administrator told her he had no idea where the report could be or whether it would have been retained after thirty-plus years.

In response to similar inquiries about the evaluation, Kimberly Bathgate of the Administrative Office of Pennsylvania Courts wrote, "We have not been able to track down an electronic version of this report."

To Sukenik, Onusic and other longtime defenders of the judge, many of the allegations against O'Kicki were never anything more than fabrications designed to discredit him as he rose to president judge and made plans to clean up corruption. Onusic said he was unfairly betrayed and abandoned by friends when he needed them most.

"I think people would be surprised to learn that he was pretty naïve about people," she said. "He really trusted in people and the goodness of people, even to the very end."

Others reject this sort of revisionist history.

According to retired Pennsylvania State Police investigator Walt Komoroski, the judge was simply good at manipulating people: "He was always working that angle—'what's in it for me?'"

Sukenik tried to sue the county for wrongful termination in 1991 with the help of attorney Neil Price. They were unsuccessful, and Price received a five-year suspension of his law license in 1999 for making unsubstantiated claims that a district judge had engaged in sexual harassment and that an assistant district attorney embezzled funds from a private client. He was also charged with filling out Department of Public Welfare forms and signing them as "Dr. Neil Price, J.D." despite having no medical license.

Others connected to the O'Kicki saga fell on hard times as well.

Rick Kirkham, who met the judge in 1990 and researched his case while reporting for an episode of *Inside Edition*, suffered from addiction and became the focal point of an anti-drug biopic called *TV Junkie*. In 2020, Kirkham was returned to the limelight as the film producer in the Netflix docuseries *Tiger King* whose footage was destroyed when Joe Exotic's zoo studio burned to the ground. Contacted via Facebook at his new home in Norway, Kirkham said he remembered little of the O'Kicki story except that he felt the judge "got screwed" in the case.

H. Clifton McWilliams—O'Kicki's predecessor as Cambria County's president judge who permitted a decade-long delay in hearing civil cases related to the 1977 Johnstown Flood—died at the age of seventy-five, just a few years after retirement. His death in 1994 occurred just before unsealed court documents revealed how Laurel Run Dam owners had ignored multiple indications that its spillway was inadequate only a year before the deadly and largely preventable deaths in Tanneryville.

Caram Abood, the former district attorney who took over for O'Kicki as president judge, sustained a long career in private practice following his resignation from the county bench amid the domestic relations office scandal. He declined through a current law partner to comment for this book. His former legal partner Dick Green died in 2004.

Richard Grifo, the senior judge from Northampton County who presided over the O'Kicki trial, was quoted in 1991 about wanting to pen a book on the case. He noted that it had widespread recognition, citing its coverage in the *Wall Street Journal*. The notion raised conflict-of-interest questions. University of Pittsburgh law professor of John Burkoff noted that lawyers are barred from signing deals with publishers amid trials and that judges have a similar code of ethics. "The literary value of a case might somehow change what that lawyer does in representation," Burkoff said. "I can see where people might have the concern over whether a judge might do something because of a book."

Edmund Spaeth Jr., a University of Pennsylvania law professor and statewide judicial reform activist, echoed Burkoff's concerns: "The paramount objective is that the judge not only be impartial, but appear impartial. If he's writing a book, I would assume he wants to sell it. Appearance is important."

Though Grifo appeared to shrug off the ethics concerns, he never published the book. He died in 2009.

O'Kicki defense attorneys Galloway and James Yelovich had long and distinguished legal careers in western Pennsylvania. Neither commented for this book. Galloway didn't return a phone call, and Yelovich—who retired in 2019—communicated through a secretary that he didn't want to be interviewed.

Onusic finished her medical education to become a board-certified and licensed nutritionist with a PhD in public health education. She ultimately returned to America, helping people "recognize the physical and mental conditions related to gluten, sensitivity, Celiac, and other food-related disorders, and how to deal with them most effectively." On occasion she travels back to Slovenia.

Lawrence Claus, who prosecuted the judge on behalf of the commonwealth, sustained a long and distinguished career. As assistant district attorney in Allegheny County, he worked to secure the convictions of the Orie sisters: Joan, a Pennsylvania Supreme Court justice; Jane, a former state senator; and a third sister who worked as a staffer. The Ories, not unlike O'Kicki, were found to have misused government resources for personal gain.

At Indiana University of Pennsylvania, there is now a Lawrence N. Claus Political Science Library Fund. Those who contribute to the Claus account help students purchase political science books, journals and online educational resources.

Claus remarked on how the case against O'Kicki created a new precedent that reverberates to this day—something called "the O'Kicki rule." He said:

> *One of the things that they had argued was statute of limitations on some of these charges for which he was convicted. And we do have what is now known as the "O'Kicki rule" interpreting statute of limitation, which means that…as long as you hold public office, you get, the commonwealth gets, an extension of time.*
>
> *If you have misdemeanors, you can prosecute someone even though eight years has passed as long as they either are still in office or have been in office within a period of time like that. And for the felonies for which he was convicted we got to go back a full thirteen years. And that was upheld by both Supreme [Court] and the Superior Court and still is the law today.*

Claus dismissed the idea that O'Kicki was just some small part of a pervasive institutional rot in Cambria County. "No, I don't think I could say that there was like a [corrupt] culture. It's just that he was Joe O'Kicki, and Joe O'Kicki had to be listened to no matter what it was that he was espousing. He was the boss," Claus said.

Krumenacker concurred. "He [claimed he] was the victim of a conspiracy. The only problem was the evidence [against him] was rather overwhelming," Krumenacker said.

"But whether it was Wid Schonek or maybe some other people he got kind of scooped up in his conspiracy theories—there was more than one, I believe—I would just attribute that to [O'Kicki's] mental deterioration."

Komoroski, who investigated O'Kicki as a member of the Pennsylvania State Police white-collar crime unit, seemed more reluctant to rule out the possibility that Cambria County's problems ran a little deeper. "I saw no evidence of what you're talking about [widespread corruption]," Komoroski said, placing special emphasis on the word "evidence."

Frederick T. Martens is even more cynical. The ex-president of both the Pennsylvania Crime Commission and the International Association for the Study of Organized Crime has investigated a staggering array of white-collar cases. He noted that former Pennsylvania attorney general Ernest Preate helped convince state legislators to defund the commonwealth's crime commission once Marten opened a probe into Preate's relationship with the Mafia and illegal gambling.

"It's systemic. What you're finding there is happening in every county in Pennsylvania," Martens said. "You keep digging into this stuff, you're going to need to shower every hour of every day just to feel clean.

"[O'Kicki] shouldn't have poked around where he poked around."

To Krumenacker and others in Cambria County, the end of the O'Kicki saga felt like a fresh start for the Ebensburg courthouse. He said:

> *I think it brought home to the judges that were sitting here at that time the need to rebuild the community's faith, that when they come up these steps and into this building that they're going to get a fair shake. That they should never, never have to worry about who's the attorney on the other side, or who's the cop on the other side...or whose politics is whose, or who's lacing somebody's pocket.*
>
> *That's why the Statue of Liberty is designed the way she is....The original had one breast bare. And the whole theory from the sculptor way back eons ago when that was developed was that a bare breast showed that there was no cover-up. That was the...artistic meaning, and the blindfold... why are they blind? Well, justice is to be blind. It doesn't matter if you're Black, white, Mexican, American, bald, short, tall...you're treated the same. And I think that was the biggest thing. It was so important, and for the bar association, too, because there were a couple attorneys that got drug into that...that we quickly...gotta clean up. And restore the faith that people would be treated fairly when they came in here.*

Ebensburg attorney Tim Burns agreed that the courthouse is currently in good hands.

"I think we should look back thirty years ago to see where we've come. I mean, you had a grand jury indict, prosecute and...eventually [convict] our president judge," Burns said.

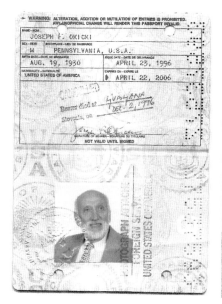

Left: Pictured is a passport issued to Joe O'Kicki on April 23, 1996. It is stamped "CANCELLED," noting that the bearer died on December 2, 1996. *Photo by Eric Kieta/ Daily American.*

Right: A look at the entrance to Zale Cemetery in Ljubljana, Slovenia. *Courtesy of Tim Burns.*

"You look at it now? Justice flows. We're quicker than many counties, but at the same time they're fair. Judges make tough decisions, but they follow the law. There's no favoritism. I read about the O'Kicki era—that's ancient history."

More than a half century since he was first elected judge, the Joe O'Kicki story still means different things to different people. It can be a tale of triumph about the son of poor immigrants; a tragedy of greed and the lives destroyed in its wake; or a series of question marks casting an immovable shadow over Cambria County.

Was the judge a plague of corruption on the courthouse? Was he a victim of those who plotted to ruin him before he could expose the wrongdoings of others in high places? Or was he perhaps a little bit of both?

"My name is 'Judge,'" O'Kicki once wrote in an incriminating letter to a bank.

It might have been hubris or arrogance. But judge or not, O'Kicki was like the rest of us. He was human.

BIBLIOGRAPHY

Altoona Mirror. "Cambria Courts Given 'Alarming' Evaluation." June 4, 1988.
———. "Framed? O'Kicki Tells National Reporter of 'Injustice." March 23, 1990.
———. "Murder Trial: Defense Seeks to Detail 'Family." March 29, 1985.
Centre Daily Times. "O'Kicki Sighting Reported in State College." March 13, 1993.
Citizens' Voice. "Judge Convicted for Abusing Power Dead at 66." February 20, 1997.
Civil action No. 3466 of 1991.
Commonwealth of Pennsylvania v. Bernard Williams.
Com. v. O'Kicki. 408 Pa. Superior Ct. 518 (1991).
Daily American. "Cambria County Officials Iron Out Differences." October 16, 1980.
———. "CTA Scandal Puts GOP in Unusual Situation." May 15, 1986.
———. "DA's Office Interviewing Witnesses." October 7, 1980.
———. "FBI Report: Rooney Had Slot-Machine Pact with Organized Crime." June 3, 1996.
———. "Friend: Judge Convicted of Abusing Power Dead at 66." February 20, 1997.
———. "Johnstown Television Company Intends to File for Channel 8." November 24, 1980.
Daily Item. "Businessman Tells of Payment." November 30, 1989.
———. "Judge Accused of Corruption." March 31, 1989.
Daily Times. "Senators Release Financial Disclosure Form." June 1, 1990.

Edmonton Journal. "Pomp, Circumstance Won't Save Judge's Fall from Grace." April 30, 1989.

Farabaugh, Patrick. *Disastrous Floods and the Demise of Steel in Johnstown.* Charleston, SC: The History Press, 2021.

———. *Water and Steel: The 1977 Johnstown Flood and the Bethlehem Steel Corporation.* N.p.: Pennsylvania Historical Association, 2019.

Indiana Gazette. "Arrest Warrant Issued for O'Kicki." March 9, 1993.

———. "Suspended Judge Sees Himself as Maverick." December 14, 1989.

Keisling, William. *Maybe Four Steps: Or, the Shame of Our Cities…The Politicalization of Our Criminal Justice System.* Yardbird Books, 1991.

Latrobe Bulletin. "Judge Requires Accountings." September 21, 1987.

———. "Justice Says Cambria Court Moves Too Slow." June 7, 1988.

———. "O'Kicki Gets 2-to-5 Years, Fines." June 28, 1990.

———. "O'Kicki Pay Ordered Stopped." May 1, 1991.

———. "State Stops Paying Salary for O'Kicki." April 24, 1991.

Mercury. "Martin Picks Schonek." October 5, 1942.

Morning Call. "O'Kicki Sightings Rival Those of Elvis." March 22, 1993.

———. "O'Kicki's Second Trial Delayed Indefinitely." December 19, 1991.

Office of Disciplinary Counsel, Petitioner, v. Neil Werner PRICE, Respondent.

O'Kicki, Joseph. "The Players." Memo.

Pennsylvania Crime Commission.

Philadelphia Inquirer. "Embattled Judge Talks about His Ascent—and His Fall." December 11, 1989.

———. "Judge Quits Lawyers Group over Rating of Candidates." May 4, 1983.

———. "Jury Hears Closing Arguments in Trial of Judge O'Kicki." December 15, 1989.

———. "O'Kicki's Trail Leads to Slovenia." March 24, 1993.

———. "O'Kicki Trial Is Delayed; Illness Cited." August 1, 1991.

———. "Preate Seeks to Halt Pay for Judge O'Kicki." April 12, 1991.

———. "State Board Asks Judge to Take Leave." October 11, 1988.

———. "Teen Gets Life Term for Telek Death." July 27, 1989.

Pittsburgh Post-Gazette. "Cambria Judge Suspended." October 12, 1988.

———. "Crime Boss John Larocca." December 4, 1984.

———. "CTA Trial: Who Are the Liars?" June 13, 1985.

———. "The Key Figures in the CTA Case." June 25, 1985.

———. "O'Kicki Saga Nears an End." July 4, 1998.

———. "O'Kicki's Wife, in Slovenia, Files for Divorce." March 11, 1993.

———. "Prosecutor Believes O'Kicki Has Fled." March 4, 1993.

———. "State Court Refuses O'Kicki Case." March 3, 1993.

Pittsburgh Press. "Ex-Judge O'Kicki Sues *Wall Street Journal* for Libel." January 29, 1991.

———. "Incline Plane Fund Begins to Climb." March 3, 1982.

———. "Johnstown Officials Tied to Rackets Here." October 30, 1971.

———. "Long Arm of Crime: Murder Trial in Cambria Shows Extent of Pittsburgh Underworld's Influence." N.d.

———. "Prosecutors Deny Pressuring Judge to Quit O'Kicki Case." September 16, 1989.

———. "Racket 'Dream' a Nightmare for Johnstown." October 31, 1971.

———. "Schonek Laughs Off Suggestion that He Started O'Kicki Inquiry." November 19, 1989.

———. "Shapp Power to Oust Racing Official Disputed." July 6, 1972.

———. "3 More Counts Dropped in Judge Hearing." May 9, 1989.

Rose, Andrew T., PhD, P.E. "The Influence of Dam Failures on Dam Safety Laws in Pennsylvania."

Schreckinger, Ben. *The Bidens: Inside the First Family's Fifty-Year Rise to Power.* New York: Hatchet Book Group, 2021

Shorto, Russell. *Smalltime: A Story of My Family and the Mob.* New York: W.W. Norton & Company, 2021.

Sixth Statewide Investigating Grand Jury Presentment.

Times-Leader (Kittanning). "New Face with New Ideas Big Need of 22nd District." October 31, 1970.

Tribune-Democrat. "Abood Postpones 36 Death Cases from '77 Flood." October 19, 1988.

———. "Brother Is Racketeer, R.C. Schonek Alleges in Lawsuit." February 6, 1989.

———. "Chums Left Out of Will." October 15, 2001.

———. "Ex-Outlaw Shot Down." May 8, 1998.

———. "Forewarned, Not Forearmed: Nearly Half of the 1977 Flood Deaths Could Have Been Prevented, Reports Show." March 19, 1995.

———. "Grim Realities of Flood Vivid at Hearing Declaring 2 Dead." July 18, 1979.

———. "Judge Writing Book about O'Kicki Trials." December 23, 1991.

———. "'Outlaw' Hearing to Go On." April 17, 1998.

———. "Outlaws: Judge Tried Extortion." April 23, 1998.

———. "Repak Indictment Is Just the Latest in Johnstown's Checkered Political Past." January 18, 2014.

———. "Victims' Families Suffered." July 20, 1997.

Tribune-Review. "Flood Cases Still Unresolved." September 16, 1984.

ABOUT THE AUTHOR

 ruce Siwy has a bachelor's in journalism from the University of Pittsburgh and works as a reporter for the *USA Today Network*'s Pennsylvania state capital bureau. His résumé includes Associated Press managing editor and Pennsylvania NewsMedia Association Professional Keystone Media awards in the spot news, sports column writing, sports, business, investigative reporting, column, enterprise reporting and podcast categories. He lives with his family in western Pennsylvania and can be found on Twitter at @BruceSiwy.